# THE WWII ORDNANCE SOLDIER'S GUIDE

by
THE ORDNANCE REPLACEMENT TRAINING CENTER * ABERDEEN PROVING GROUNDS * MARYLAND

RESTRICTED

©2013 Periscope Film LLC
All Rights Reserved
ISBN#978-1-937684-18-1
www.PeriscopeFilm.com

# TO THE NEW ORDNANCE SOLDIER

The fighting Ordnance Soldier is a new development of this war. In earlier wars the Ordnance man was primarily a technical expert. Now he combines technical skill with military capacity to defend himself and even to attack the enemy if necessary. Ordnance Soldiers have already been in a number of battles. You must therefore know the basic art of war. Your first objective is to become a fighting man, tough physically, skilled with the rifle and other weapons, knowing how to conserve your life by adequate field fortifications and by sound sanitary precautions, and by ability to treat yourself and your fellow soldiers for wounds or broken limbs. Then the paratroopers, the tanks that break through, the dive bombers will have no terrors for you.

When you have learned these things, the science of the Ordnance Soldier must be acquired. Each man will be given training in a technical skill that is used on the battlefield to keep the fighting tools of the U.S. Army supplied and in good operating condition.

Learning how to fulfill this mission is a never-ending process. It is to help you learn your job that the ORDNANCE SOLDIER'S GUIDE has been prepared. It contains practical tips drawn from actual battle experience and technical data from the latest Army publications.

This copy is yours. Take it to all your training periods. Take notes in it and study them in your spare time.

---

THE ORDNANCE REPLACEMENT TRAINING CENTER

ABERDEEN PROVING GROUND, MD.

# INDEX

| | |
|---|---|
| Ammunition | 83 |
| Ammunition Supply | 75 |
| Articles of War | 6 |
| Artificial Respiration | 29 |
| Artillery | 89 |
| Automotive | 94 |
| Block and Tackle | 56 |
| Booby Traps | 64 |
| Camouflage | 38 |
| Care and Cleaning of Clothing and Equipment | 14 |
| Clerks | 100 |
| Defense Against Air and Paratroop Attack | 48 |
| Defense Against Chemical Attack | 31 |
| Defense Against Mechanized Attack | 42 |
| Demolitions | 62 |
| Division, The | 11 |
| Fire Control Instruments | 104 |
| First Aid | 26 |
| General Orders | 17 |
| Glossary | 119 |
| Grenades | 46 |
| Hand to Hand Combat - "Kill" | 68 |
| Hasty Field Fortifications | 36 |
| Hoisting Devices | 57 |
| Identification of Aircraft | 49 |
| Insignia, Commissioned Officers | 12 |
| Insignia, Non-Commissioned Officers | 13 |
| Interior Guard | 16 |
| Introduction | 1 |
| Knots and Hitches | 55 |
| Malaria | 24 |
| Map (Pre-War Europe and Asia) | 118 |
| Map Reading | 50 |
| Message Communication | 61 |
| Military Courtesy | 4 |
| Military Sanitation | 23 |
| Mines and Minefields | 44 |
| Missions of Various Branches | 10 |
| Motor Vehicle Operation | 98 |
| Ordnance Materiel | 73 |
| Ordnance Service in the Field | 74 |
| Organization of Army | 8 |
| Organization of The Office Chief of Ordnance | 72 |
| Rifle Marksmanship | 18 |
| Safeguarding Military Information | 3 |
| Shops Trucks | 108 |
| Scouting and Patrolling | 58 |
| Small Arms | 76 |
| Sources of Information | 102 |
| The War, How It Started | 116 |
| Tips From an Old Top Kick | 114 |
| Uniform Identification | 111 |

# SAFEGUARDING MILITARY INFORMATION

You will notice the word "Restricted" on the cover of the GUIDE. Restricted military information will not be communicated to the public or to the press, but may be given to any person known to be in the service of the United States and to persons of undoubted loyalty and discretion who are cooperating in government work. That means that you shouldn't discuss the contents of the GUIDE with a friendly citizen who buys you a beer, or a fellow train passenger. Don't discuss troop movements with anybody at any time! The most seemingly innocent comments may easily cost your life or the lives of your comrades.

1. "WELL...REGIMENT SAILS FRIDAY..."

2. "REGIMENT SAILS FRIDAY..."

3. "SAILS FRIDAY...."

4. **FRIDAY!**

5.

# MILITARY COURTESY

When a medieval knight met a fellow man-of-arms, he approached with his steel helmet closed, for every man was a potential enemy. Upon recognition, however, he raised the visor - a token of confidence. That gesture of the hand has been carried down through the centuries to become the military salute of today.

Being polite and considerate towards others, either civilian or military, whether junior or senior, is courtesy. The salute, the most important of all military courtesies is not a mark of subservience, but an indication of the possession of military courtesy and discipline by those rendering it. Its omission indicates a lack of courtesy - a mark of poor discipline.

The salute is rendered by raising your right hand smartly until the tip of your forefinger (index finger) touches the brim of your headdress, above and slightly to the right of your right eye. If you are without cap or hat, the tip of your forefinger touches your forehead above and slightly to the right of your right eye. In either case you keep your thumb and fingers extended and joined, palm to the left and the hand and wrist straight. You also keep your upper arm horizontal and the forearm inclined at an angle of 45°. At the same time, you turn your head and eyes toward the person you are saluting. The second part of this movement consists in dropping your arm to your side and turning your head and eyes to the front.

RIFLE SALUTE

PRESENT ARMS

AT RIGHT SHOULDER ARMS

AT ORDER ARMS AND AT TRAIL ARMS

# WHEN TO SALUTE

### 1. REPORTING TO COMPANY COMMANDER

Receive permission of the First Sergeant to speak to the Company Commander whenever you have urgent business that requires his attention.

Knock on the Company Commander's door and wait until you are asked to come in. Enter, halt two paces from the Company Commander's desk and salute.

Complete salute and report: "Sir, Pvt._____ has the First Sergeant's permission to speak to the Company Commander" or "Sir, Pvt._____ reports to the Company Commander".

Finishing conversation, salute and leave the office by executing an about face.

### 2. AT RETREAT

At Retreat and not in formation, at the first note of music, face toward the colors, stand at attention and salute. When driving a vehicle, you are required to stop, dismount, face the flag, and salute.

### 3. REPORTING TO AN OFFICER OUT OF DOORS

Halt at least two paces from the officer, salute, and state: "Sir, Pvt._____ reports to Captain _____."

While talking, stand at attention. When the conversation is over, salute, about face and depart.

When reporting to or passing an officer while you are carrying a rifle, execute the rifle salute.

### 4. WHEN RUNNING

When running come down to a walk before saluting.

### 5. WHEN POSTED AS A SENTINEL

Sentinels posted with a rifle salute by presenting arms.

### 6. PASSING AN OFFICER

The salute should be given when you can easily recognize that the person is an officer entitled to it.

The distance is usually between 6 and 30 paces. Beyond 30 paces the officer is not easily recognizable as such; within 6 paces the officer does not have time to return the salute.
NOTE: When walking with an officer walk at his left. Remove cigarette or pipe from the right hand or mouth before saluting.

### 7. AT PAY TABLE

At Pay Table, enter when your name is called, salute, and give your name to the Officer. When you receive your pay, do not salute again, but leave by the shortest route.

# ARTICLES OF WAR

While our country is at war the following crimes are important because of the increased seriousness of the offenses. The Articles of War applying to each crime, the maximum punishment, and the necessary elements, constituting the crime itself are stated below:

| ARTICLE OF WAR | CRIME | MAXIMUM PUNISHMENT | CIRCUMSTANCE |
|---|---|---|---|
| 58 | Desertion | Death | AWOL plus intent not to return, which may be inferred. AWOL to shirk hazardous duty or important service (See Article of War 28) |
| 59 | Advising or aiding another to desert | Death | Any advice or assistance to a deserter |
| 61 | Absence without leave | Life imprisonment | Absence from command, guard, quarters, station or camp for ANY length of time (one minute or more) |
| 63 | Disrespect toward a superior officer | Confinement at hard labor for six months and forfeiture of two-thirds pay per month for six months | Disrespect by words or gestures |
| 64 | Assaulting or willfully disobeying a superior officer | Death | Any willful disobedience or assault which may be inferred from the circumstances |
| 65 | Insubordination, disobedience, assault, or disrespect towards a Warrant Officer or non-commissioned officer | Confinement at hard labor for six months and forfeiture of two-thirds pay per month for six months | A deliberate act by word or gesture |
| 66 | Mutiny or Sedition | Death | Defiance of or resistance to lawful military authority of two or more military personnel with intent to usurp or override such authority |
| 67 | Failure to suppress Mutiny or Sedition | Death | Failure to suppress, or withholding information of a mutiny |
| 75 | Misbehavior before the enemy | Death | Running away from scene of battle, abandoning, or by misconduct or neglect, endangering the safety of other military personnel |

| | | | |
|---|---|---|---|
| 76 | Subordinates trying to compel their superiors to surrender | Death | Any compulsion or attempt to compel any commander of any garrison, fort, post, camp, or guard to surrender same |
| 77 | Improper use of countersign | Death | Telling password to unauthorized persons or falsifying it to authorized persons |
| 78 | Forcing a safeguard | Death | Attempting to pass a military guard when challenged without showing credentials |
| 81 | Aiding the Enemy | Death | By word of mouth or deed |
| 82 | Spying for the Enemy | Death (mandatory) | Lurking about or spying in/or about fortifications, posts, quarters or encampments |
| 83 | Loss or damage thru neglect or improper disposition of property | Dishonorable Discharge, two years confinement at hard labor, forfeiture of all pay | Willful act which may be inferred from the circumstances |
| 84 | Wasteful or unlawful disposition of military property issued to soldiers | Dishonorable Discharge, five years confinement at hard labor, forfeiture of all pay | Willful act which may be inferred from the circumstances |
| 85 | Drunk on duty | Confinement at hard labor for six months and forfeiture of two-thirds pay per month for six months | Not in control of physical and mental faculties |
| 86 | Misbehavior of Sentinel | Death | Drunk or sleeping on guard duty |
| 92 | Murder or Rape | Death | Willful act which may be inferred from the circumstances |
| 93 | Various crimes (arson, assault, forgery, manslaughter, perjury, sodomy, etc) | Dishonorable Discharge, twenty years confinement at hard labor, forfeiture of all pay | Willful act which may be inferred from the circumstances |
| 94 | Frauds against the Government | Dishonorable Discharge, five years confinement at hard labor, forfeiture of all pay | Unlawful acts for deeds which may be inferred from the circumstances |
| 96 | All crimes not specifically covered by other Articles of War | Dishonorable Discharge, five years confinement at hard labor, forfeiture of all pay | By act, deeds, or gestures |
| 104 | Company Punishment | One week extra fatigue or substitutions thereof not to exceed one week | Minor offenses not involving moral turpitude |

# ORGANIZATION OF ARMY

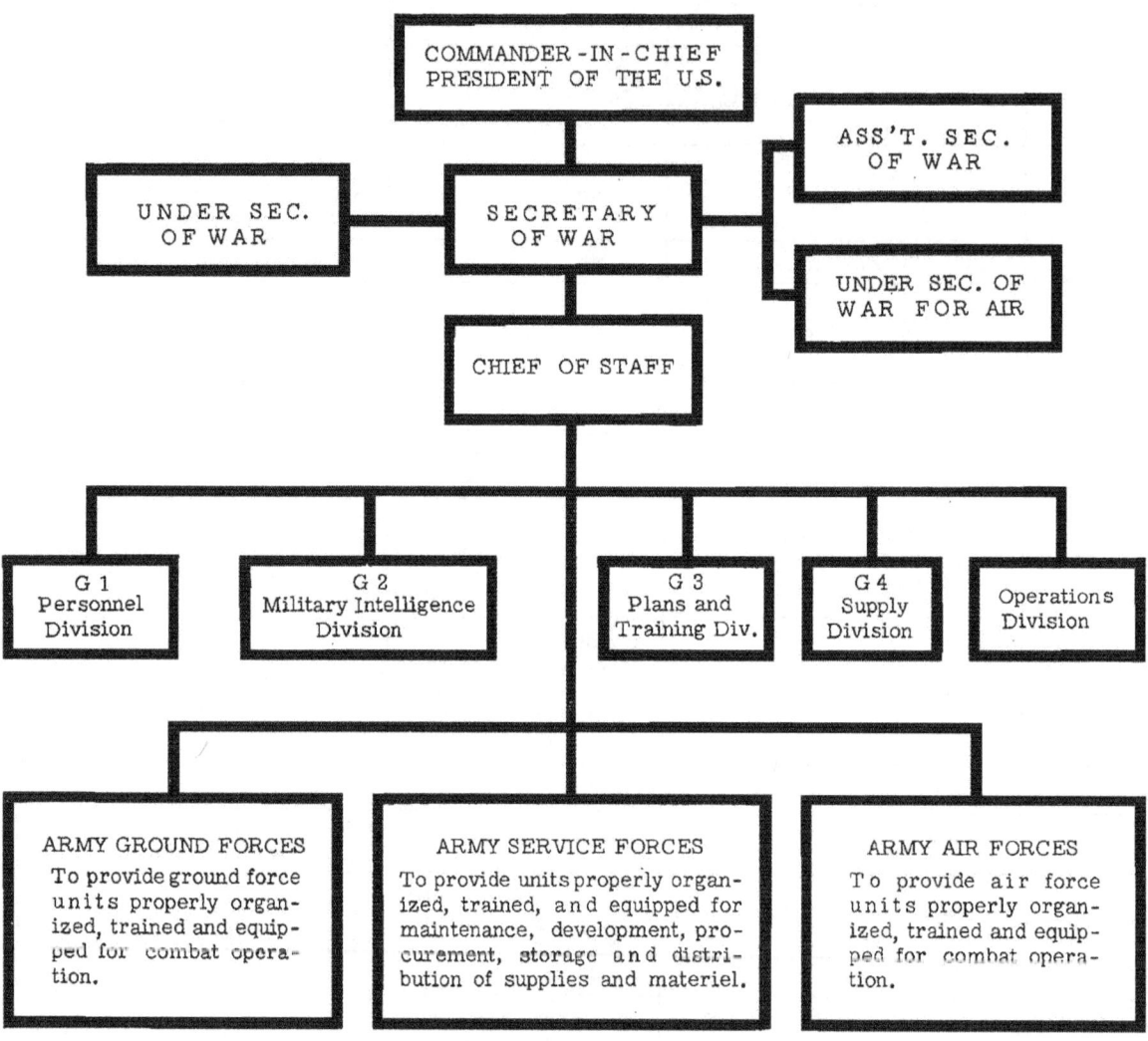

## CHAIN OF COMMAND

CHAIN OF COMMAND extends from the corporal who leads a squad, through the sergeants and officers in command of the larger units, to the President of the United States, the commander-in-chief of our armed forces.

| TACTICAL UNIT | APPROX. NO. OF MEN | COMMANDER |
|---|---|---|
| Squad | 12 | Corporal |
| Platoon | 50 | Lieutenant |
| Company | 200 | Captain |
| Battalion (Inf.) | 900 | Major |
| Regiment (Inf.) | 3,200 | Colonel |
| Division | 15,000 | Major General |
| Corps | 75,000 | Lt. General |
| Army | 300,000 | General |

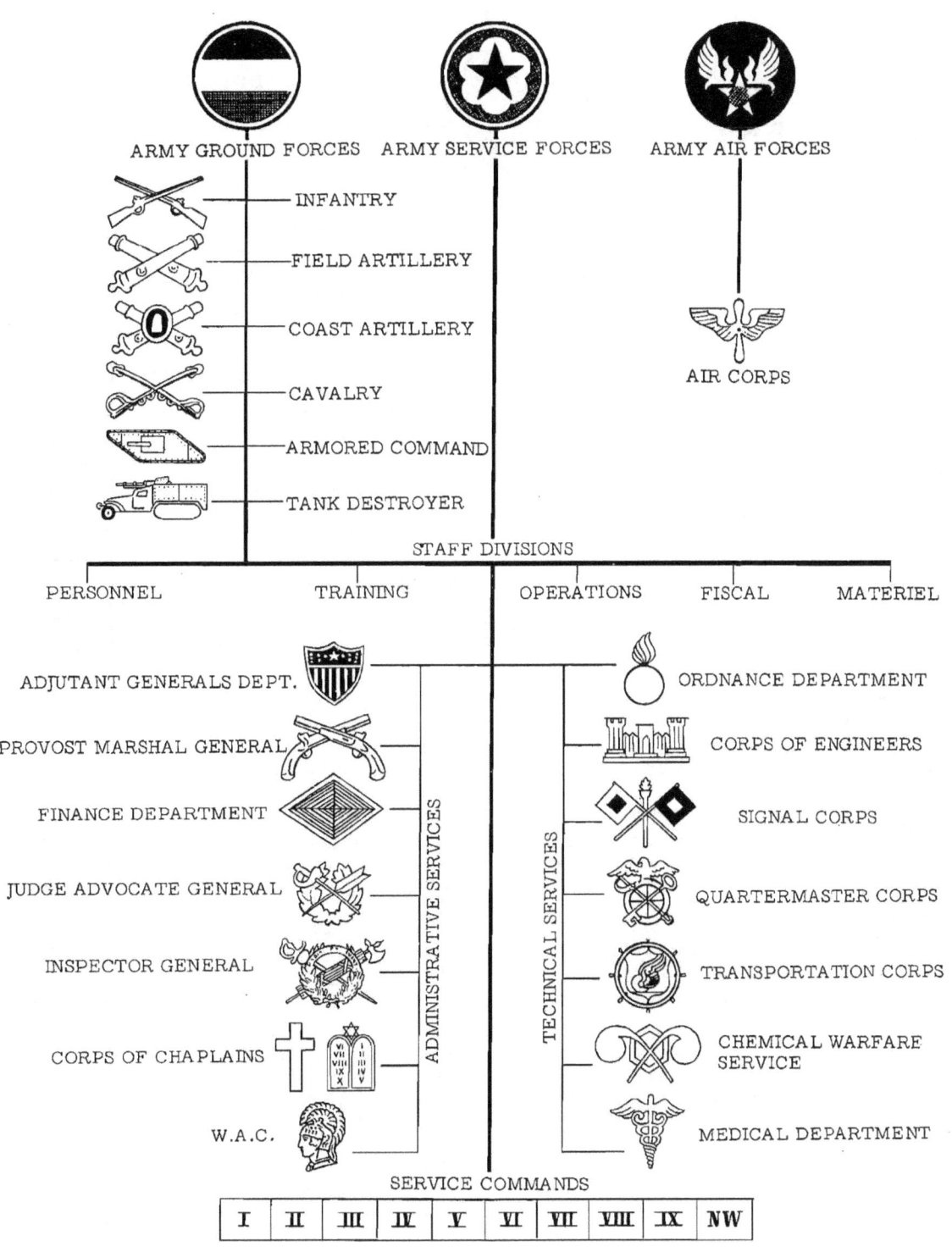

# MISSIONS OF VARIOUS BRANCHES

GENERAL STAFF:
Aids Secretary of War in forming and executing plans and policies for the entire army.

 INFANTRY:
A fighting arm — supported by other arms. Chief weapons: mortars, rifles and machine guns.

ORDNANCE DEPARTMENT:
Designs, procures, issues and maintains weapons, motor vehicles, and ammunition.

 CAVALRY:
Horse and mechanized. Used for attack, reconnaissance, security. Weapons like that of Infantry.

QUARTERMASTER CORPS:
Feeds, clothes, and houses the Army. Procures all material of standard manufacture.

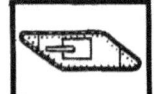 ARMORED COMMAND:
Tanks furnish greatest striking power of attack. Have greatest mobility and fire power.

CHEMICAL WARFARE SERVICE:
Protects against enemy chemicals; may support fighting arms in retaliatory gas warfare.

 TANK DESTROYER COMMAND:
Operates against and destroys enemy armored forces. Has high fire power and mobility.

TRANSPORTATION CORPS:
Embraces rail, water, highway shipments; ports of embarkation, regulating stations.

 FIELD ARTILLERY:
Supports Infantry and Cavalry with guns, howitzers. Firing unit is battery of four guns.

MEDICAL DEPARTMENT:
Maintains health of Army. Services: medical, dental, sanitary, nursing, veterinary.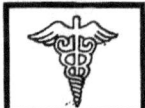

 COAST ARTILLERY:
Operates coast guns, mines ports, charged with all antiaircraft defense.

FINANCE DEPARTMENT:
Pays Army salaries and amounts due for Army purchases. Audits accounts of Army property.

 ARMY AIR FORCES:
Missions: bombardment, pursuit, observation, air defense, ground support, and transport.

ADJUTANT GENERAL'S DEPT:
Communicates orders. Arranges and preserves military records. Conducts recruiting service.

 CORPS OF ENGINEERS:
Builds roads, bridges. Charged with laying mines, camouflage, demolitions, operation of utilities.

CORPS OF CHAPLAINS:
Is specially charged with religious, and moral welfare of members of all arms and services.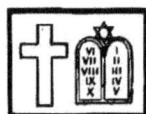

 SIGNAL CORPS:
Handles all signal communications at headquarters of divisions and larger units.

INSPECTOR GENERAL'S OFFICE
Assists in military administration. Inspects commands, posts and installations. Investigates complaints.

# THE DIVISION

The Infantry Division is the basic organization of the field forces. It is composed of all the essential ground arms and services and can conduct, by its own means, operations of general importance. It can act alone or as a part of a higher unit.

The Airborne Division is about two-thirds the size of the Infantry Division. In addition to rifles and machine guns, it carries rocket launchers, mortars, 37 or 40-mm guns, and 75-mm howitzers.

The Light Infantry Division is considerably smaller than the regular division, but has approximately the same fire power in small arms and automatic weapons. It is designed especially for amphibious, airborne, mountain, and jungle operations, equipment varying with the type of operations. (Tentative)

The Armored Division is a powerfully armed and armored, highly mobile force. Its outstanding characteristics are its battlefield mobility and its protected fire power. The Armored Division is organized primarily to perform missions that require great mobility and firepower. Its primary role is in offensive operations against hostile rear areas.

# INSIGNIA, COMMISSIONED OFFICERS AND WARRANT OFFICERS

Rank Insignia on cap.

U.S. without background on upper lapels.

Branch Insignia without background on lower lapels.

Regimental Insignia on shoulder straps.

Rank Insignia on shoulder straps.

GENERAL

LIEUTENANT GENERAL

MAJOR GENERAL

BRIGADIER GENERAL

COLONEL

LIEUTENANT COLONEL

MAJOR (Gold)

CAPTAIN

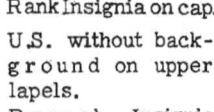
1st LIEUTENANT

2nd LIEUTENANT (Gold)

CHIEF WARRANT OFFICER
(Brown with Gold Band)

WARRANT OFFICER (J.G.)
(Brown with Gold Band)

# INSIGNIA, NON-COMMISSIONED OFFICERS AND ENLISTED PERSONNEL

Regimental Insignia on cap.

U.S. with background on upper right lapel.

Branch Insignia with background on upper left lapel.

Regimental Insignia on lower lapels.

Chevrons of rank on sleeves.

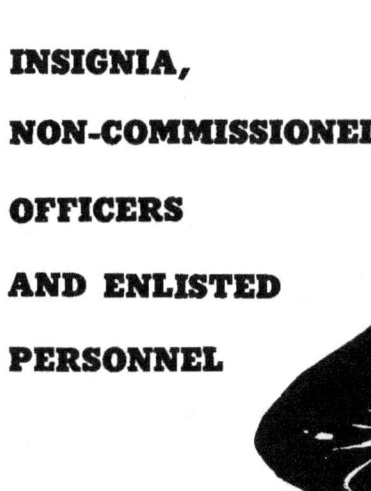

FIRST SERGEANT    MASTER SERGEANT

TECHNICAL SERGEANT    STAFF SERGEANT     TECHNICIAN 3rd GRADE    SERGEANT

 TECHNICIAN 4th GRADE     CORPORAL     TECHNICIAN 5th GRADE     PRIVATE FIRST CLASS

# CARE AND CLEANING OF CLOTHING AND EQUIPMENT

RESPONSIBILITY FOR PROPERTY: Clothing and equipment issued to you are government property. If any articles are lost or damaged through your fault or negligence you will be required to pay for them. If you were responsible for the loss or damage, through fault or negligence, then you should admit that fact by signing a "Statement of Charges." If, however, you believe that you were not responsible, do not sign this statement. In the latter case a "Report of Survey" will be made out and a Surveying Officer will determine whether or not you are to be held responsible. When articles of clothing or equipment have become worn out through ordinary wear and tear, no one is held responsible for the value and the worn articles may be exchanged for new ones.

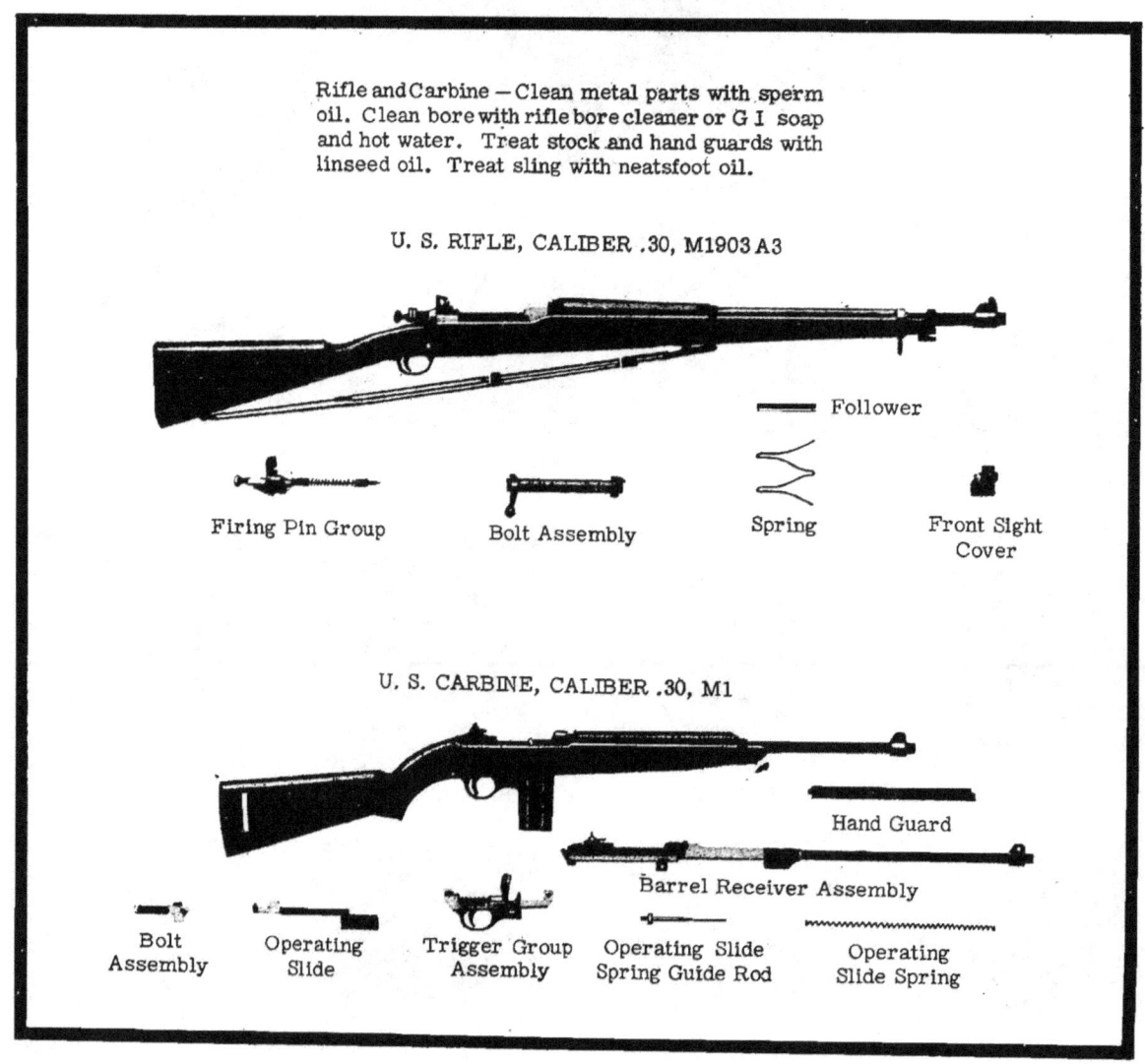

### LEATHER
Use mild soap and warm water to clean shoes. Apply saddle soap and dry slowly. Use dubbing to waterproof shoes.

### WEB
Wash with mild soap and warm water. Dry thoroughly in a place away from the sun.

### CLOTHING
Have clothing altered if necessary. Have available a small sewing kit, a can of cleaning solvent, and equipment for pressing clothes.

### GAS MASK
1. Keep it clean, dry and adjusted to fit your head.
2. After wearing it, wipe it dry thoroughly.
3. At least once a week, examine it for damage, put it on and test it, then wash it with soap and water and dry it carefully.

### MESS GEAR
Wash with soap and hot water. A few pebbles inside the canteen will assist in cleaning.

### CARE OF TENTING EQUIPMENT
Do not hammer pegs into hard ground. Brush and dry canvas thoroughly before folding and storing. Wash thoroughly and dry before storing.

### BRASS
Clean with polishing cloth, soap and water. Shine with soft rag.

# DISPLAY OF FIELD EQUIPMENT

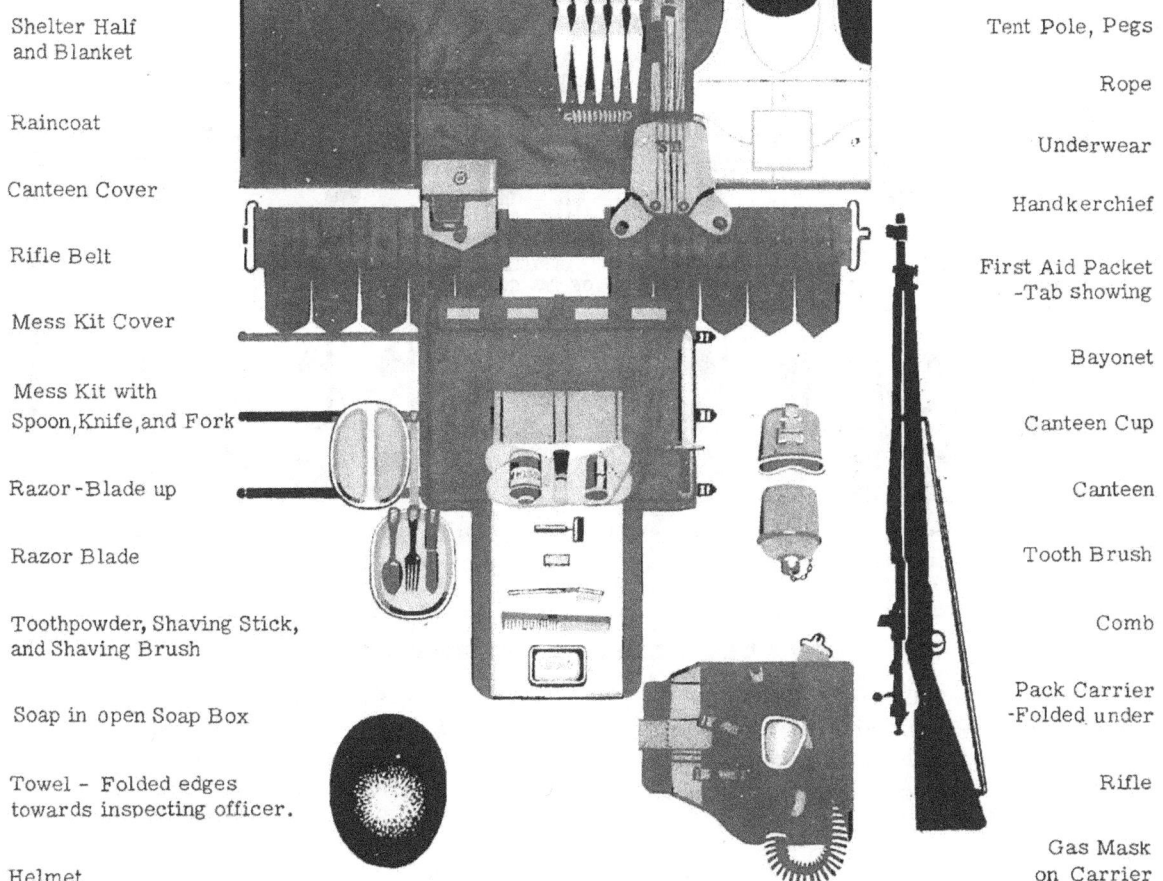

Shelter Half and Blanket

Raincoat

Canteen Cover

Rifle Belt

Mess Kit Cover

Mess Kit with Spoon, Knife, and Fork

Razor - Blade up

Razor Blade

Toothpowder, Shaving Stick, and Shaving Brush

Soap in open Soap Box

Towel - Folded edges towards inspecting officer.

Helmet

Tent Pole, Pegs

Rope

Underwear

Handkerchief

First Aid Packet -Tab showing

Bayonet

Canteen Cup

Canteen

Tooth Brush

Comb

Pack Carrier -Folded under

Rifle

Gas Mask on Carrier

# INTERIOR GUARD

PURPOSES: 1._____  2._____  3._____

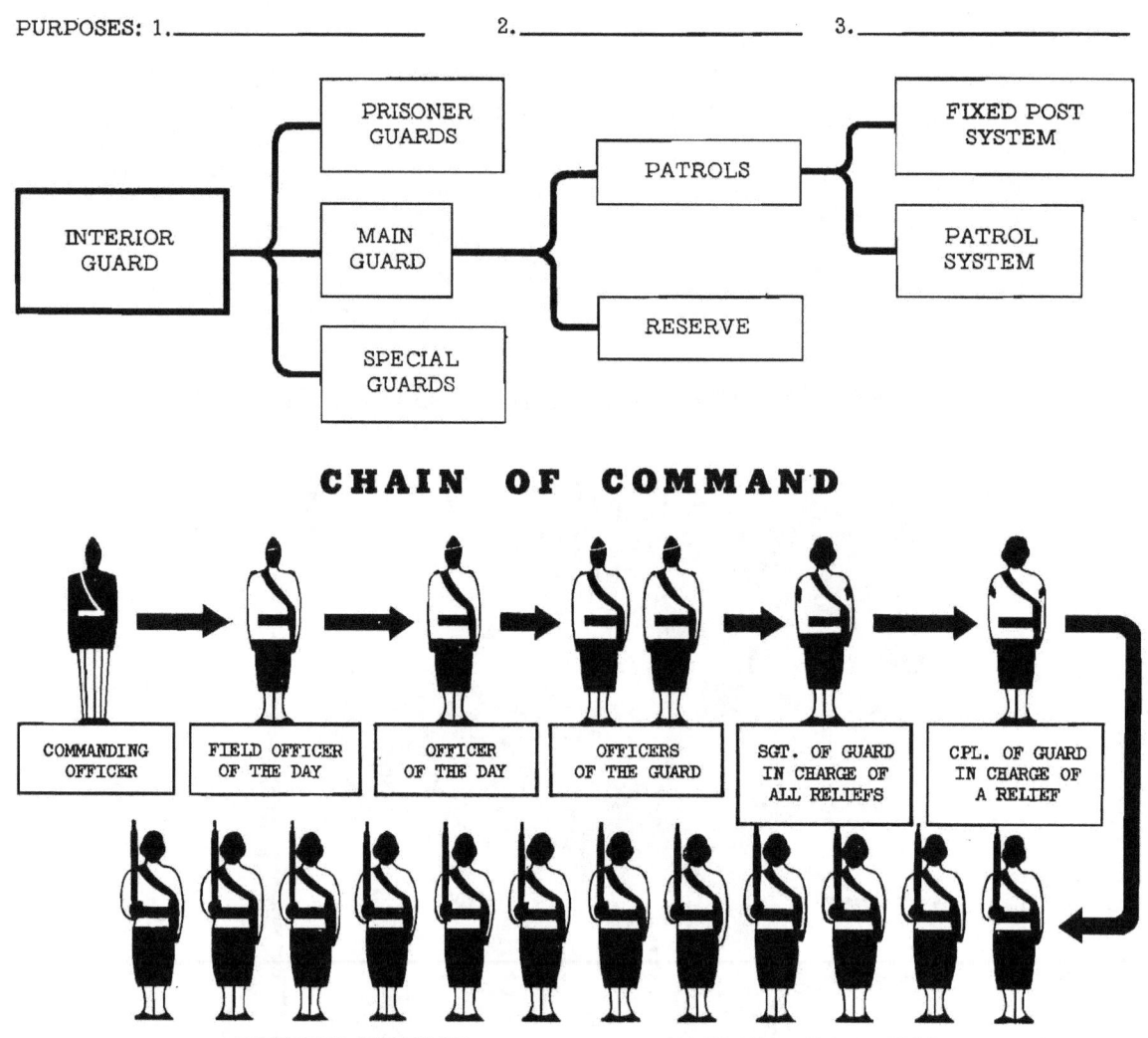

## CHAIN OF COMMAND

PRIVATES OF GUARD          EACH PATROLS A POST

| CHALLENGING PROCEDURE | | | |
|---|---|---|---|
| SENTRY: | (At 30 Paces) "Halt! Who is there?" | | (Soldier advances) |
| PARTY: | "Soldier of the post." | SENTRY: | (At 6 paces) "Halt!" |
| SENTRY: | "Advance, soldier of the post, to be recognized." | | (Recognizes soldier) |
| | | SENTRY: | "Advance, soldier of the post." (Soldier goes on his way) |

# GENERAL ORDERS:

### 1. TO TAKE
To take charge of this post and all government property in view.

### 2. TO WALK
To walk my post in a military manner, keeping always on the alert and observing everything that takes place within sight or hearing.

### 3. TO REPORT
To report all violations of orders I am instructed to enforce.

### 4. TO REPEAT
To repeat all calls from posts more distant from the guardhouse than my own.

### 5. TO QUIT
To quit my post only when properly relieved.

### 6. TO RECEIVE
To receive, obey, and pass on to the sentinel who relieves me all orders from the commanding officer, officer of the day, and officers and noncommissioned officers of the guard only.

### 7. TO TALK
To talk to no one except in line of duty.

### 8. TO GIVE
To give the alarm in case of fire or disorder.

### 9. TO CALL
To call the corporal of the guard in any case not covered by instructions.

### 10. TO SALUTE
To salute all officers and all colors and standards not cased.

### 11. TO BE
To be especially watchful at night and during the time for challenging, to challenge all persons on or near my post, and to allow no one to pass without proper authority.

Wherever an American soldier walks guard under the Stars and Stripes, whether it be in the United States or some far-flung combat zone, his actions are prescribed by the General Orders. Special Orders, on the other hand, apply to only one guard post.

# EMERGENCY CALLS:

"CORPORAL OF THE GUARD, NO. 13!"

"CORPORAL OF THE GUARD, NO. 13, RELIEF!"

"THE GUARD, NO. 13!"

"FIRE, NO. 13!"

# RIFLE MARKSMANSHIP

SIGHTING AND AIMING
Aligning of sights

FRONT SIGHT

PEEP SIGHT

PROPER ALIGNING

POSITION OF BULLS-EYE

## THE SLING

KEEPER — FROG — UPPER LOOP — KEEPER — LOWER LOOP

LOOP SLING

1. Loosen lower frog and fasten near butt swivel.
2. Give sling 1/2 turn to left.
3. Insert arm through upper loop.

4. Upper loop is near the shoulder and well above the biceps muscle.
5. Pull keepers and frog close to arm.

6. Move left hand over top of sling.
7. Sling lies smoothly along hand and wrist.
8. Bring rifle into firing position.

HASTY SLING

1. Loosen lower loop.

2. Throw sling to left 1/2 turn and catch it above the elbow and high on the arm.

3. Bring rifle into firing position.

# INDIVIDUAL SAFETY PRECAUTIONS

1. Consider every rifle to be loaded until you have examined it and proved it to be unloaded.

6. Do not let the firing pin down by hand on a cartridge in the chamber.

2. Never point the rifle at anyone you do not intend to kill, nor in a direction where an accidental discharge may do harm.

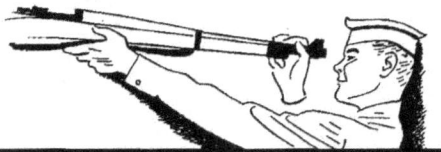

7. Be sure that the rifle is clean and dry before firing. Remove all traces of oil or dust.

3. Always unload the rifle if it is to be left where someone else may handle it.

8. Never grease or oil the ammunition or the walls of the rifle chamber --- clean rifle before firing.

4. Always point the rifle up when snapping the trigger after inspection.

9. See that the ammunition is clean and dry --- examine all live and dummy ammunition.

5. Keep safety lock on when there is a cartridge in the chamber.

10. Keep ammunition from direct rays of the sun.

11. Keep the bolt open when not using rifle on the firing line.

# FIRING POSITIONS

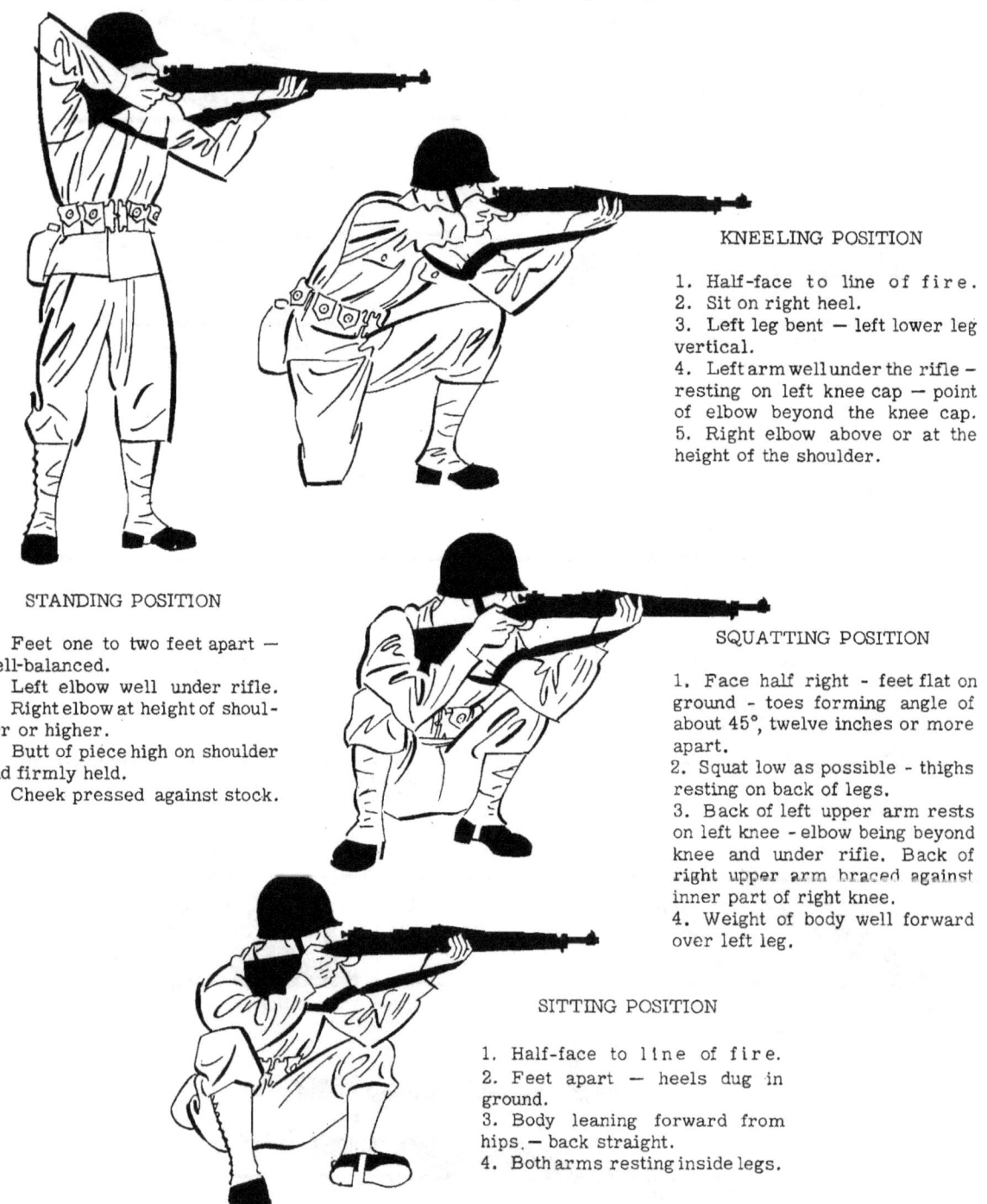

KNEELING POSITION

1. Half-face to line of fire.
2. Sit on right heel.
3. Left leg bent — left lower leg vertical.
4. Left arm well under the rifle - resting on left knee cap — point of elbow beyond the knee cap.
5. Right elbow above or at the height of the shoulder.

STANDING POSITION

1. Feet one to two feet apart — well-balanced.
2. Left elbow well under rifle.
3. Right elbow at height of shoulder or higher.
4. Butt of piece high on shoulder and firmly held.
5. Cheek pressed against stock.

SQUATTING POSITION

1. Face half right - feet flat on ground - toes forming angle of about 45°, twelve inches or more apart.
2. Squat low as possible - thighs resting on back of legs.
3. Back of left upper arm rests on left knee - elbow being beyond knee and under rifle. Back of right upper arm braced against inner part of right knee.
4. Weight of body well forward over left leg.

SITTING POSITION

1. Half-face to line of fire.
2. Feet apart — heels dug in ground.
3. Body leaning forward from hips.— back straight.
4. Both arms resting inside legs.

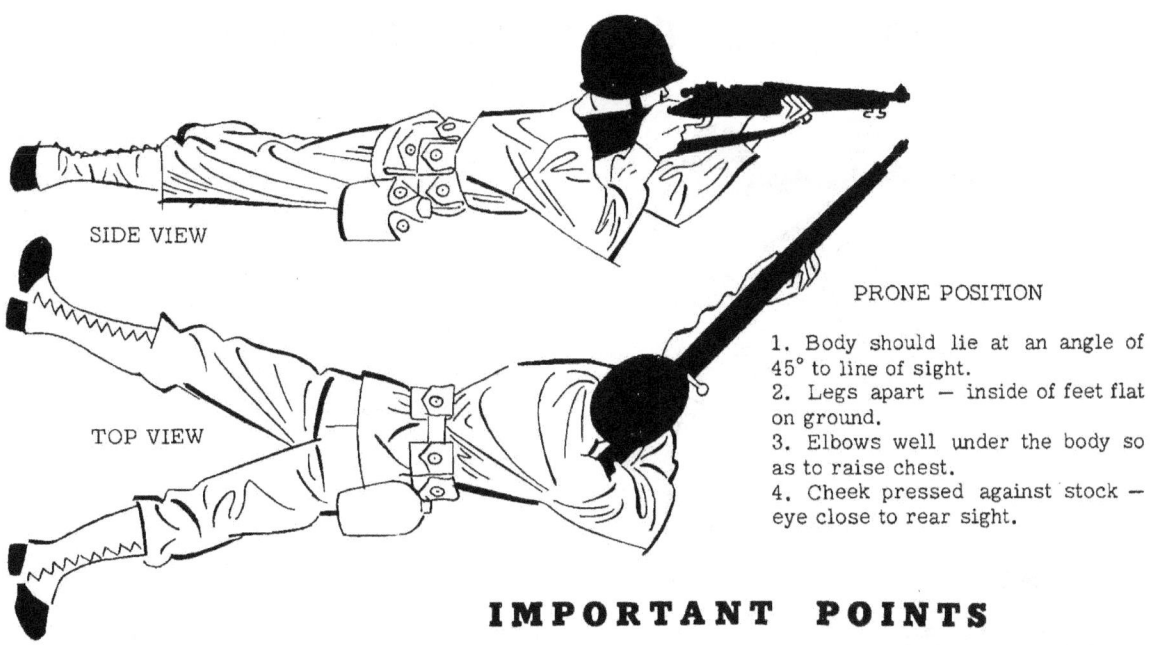

### PRONE POSITION

1. Body should lie at an angle of 45° to line of sight.
2. Legs apart — inside of feet flat on ground.
3. Elbows well under the body so as to raise chest.
4. Cheek pressed against stock — eye close to rear sight.

## IMPORTANT POINTS

1. Keep sling properly adjusted — tight enough to give support — high up on arm.
2. Assume proper position.
3. Take up slack in trigger promptly.
4. Sight and aim correctly, keeping eye always on the target.
5. Hold breath while aiming and SQUEEZE the trigger so that you do not know when the piece will be discharged. Follow thru, squeezing the trigger after shot has been fired.

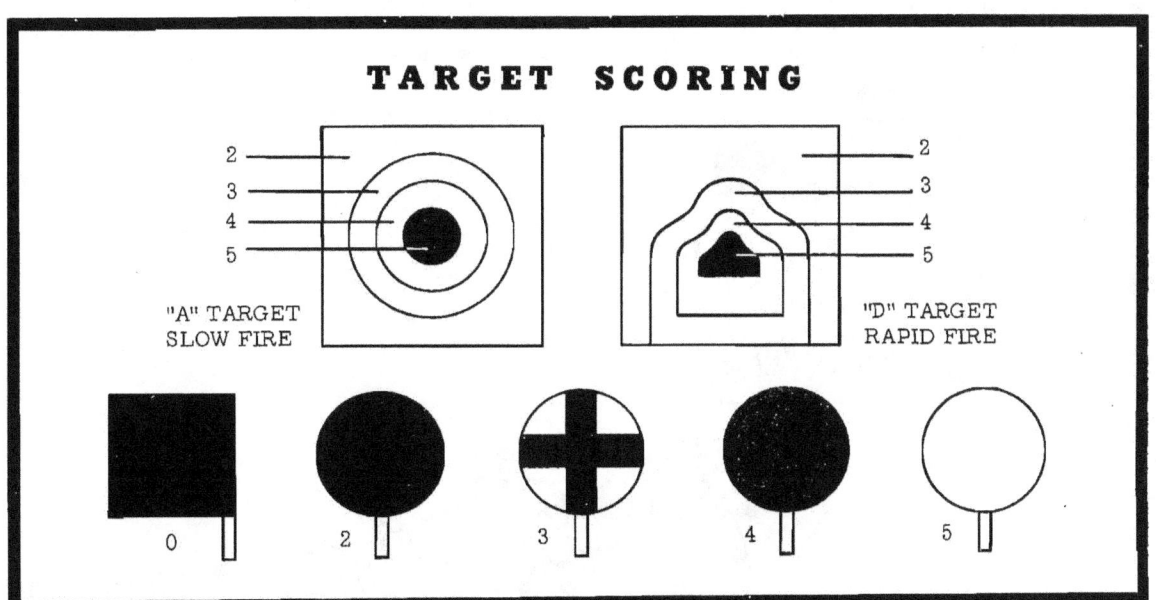

# DUTIES OF THE COACH

On the firing line the coach will take a position similar to that of the man who is firing — prone, sitting, kneeling, standing, squatting — so as to be able to watch his trigger finger and his eye. The coach observes the pupil carefully and corrects all errors. He pays particular attention to see that —

1. The sights are blackened and that they are set at the correct range.

2. The ammunition is free from dirt.

3. The pupil has the correct position, gun sling properly adjusted, body at proper angle, elbows correctly placed and the cheek pressed firmly against the stock.

4. The slack is taken up promptly.

5. The trigger is squeezed properly.

6. The pupil fires without flinching (watch his eye).

7. The pupil calls his shot each time he fires.

8. The pupil keeps his score book correctly.

9. The pupil is holding his breath properly (by watching his back occasionally). If the pupil spends more than six or eight seconds in aiming and holding his breath, have him start again.

10. The pupil shoots well. If not, have him fire a few "dry shots", checking his eye and follow through.

During sustained fire, the coach will pay attention, in addition to the above, to see that —

1. The bolt is working rapidly.

2. While working the bolt the pupil keeps his eye on the target, the rifle to his shoulder, and his elbows in place. Watch the man's eye, not the target. If you detect the pupil closing his eye, he is doing it before the explosion. Caution him to follow through, relax, keep looking, and not to force it.

3. The magazine is reloaded from a clip properly and quickly.

# MILITARY SANITATION

### GENERAL RULES OF PERSONAL HYGIENE

1. Insure internal cleanliness by proper chewing of food, and by drinking plenty of water.
2. Take care of your feet by alternating the wearing of your shoes. Wear clean, dry socks. Do not wear worn-out or mended socks — turn them in for salvage. Use foot baths and foot powder.
3. Bathe your body at least twice weekly. Pay particular attention to armpits, crotch, and feet.
4. Brush your teeth at least twice daily. Take advantage of free dental facilities on your post.
5. Insure proper hair hygiene by washing your hair at least once a week. Visit your barber shop frequently. Long, dirty hair is an excellent breeding place for lice.
6. Wear clean clothes. It is to no avail to take a bath and then don a dirty uniform.
7. Get at least 7 hours sleep in a well ventilated room.

### METHODS OF WATER PURIFICATION

| BOILING | CALCIUM HYPOCHLORITE | | TABLETS |
|---------|----------------------|---|---------|
|         | Capsule | Lyster Bag<br>Ampule | 2 to 4 |

CHLORINATION TEST _____

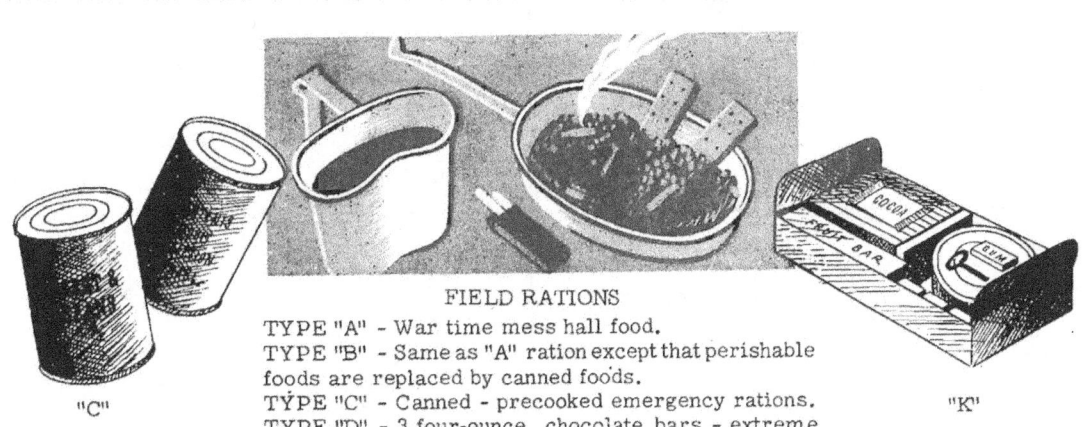

### FIELD RATIONS

TYPE "A" - War time mess hall food.
TYPE "B" - Same as "A" ration except that perishable foods are replaced by canned foods.
TYPE "C" - Canned - precooked emergency rations.
TYPE "D" - 3 four-ounce, chocolate bars - extreme emergency ration.
TYPE "K" - Prepared foods packed in cardboard containers. Emergency ration.

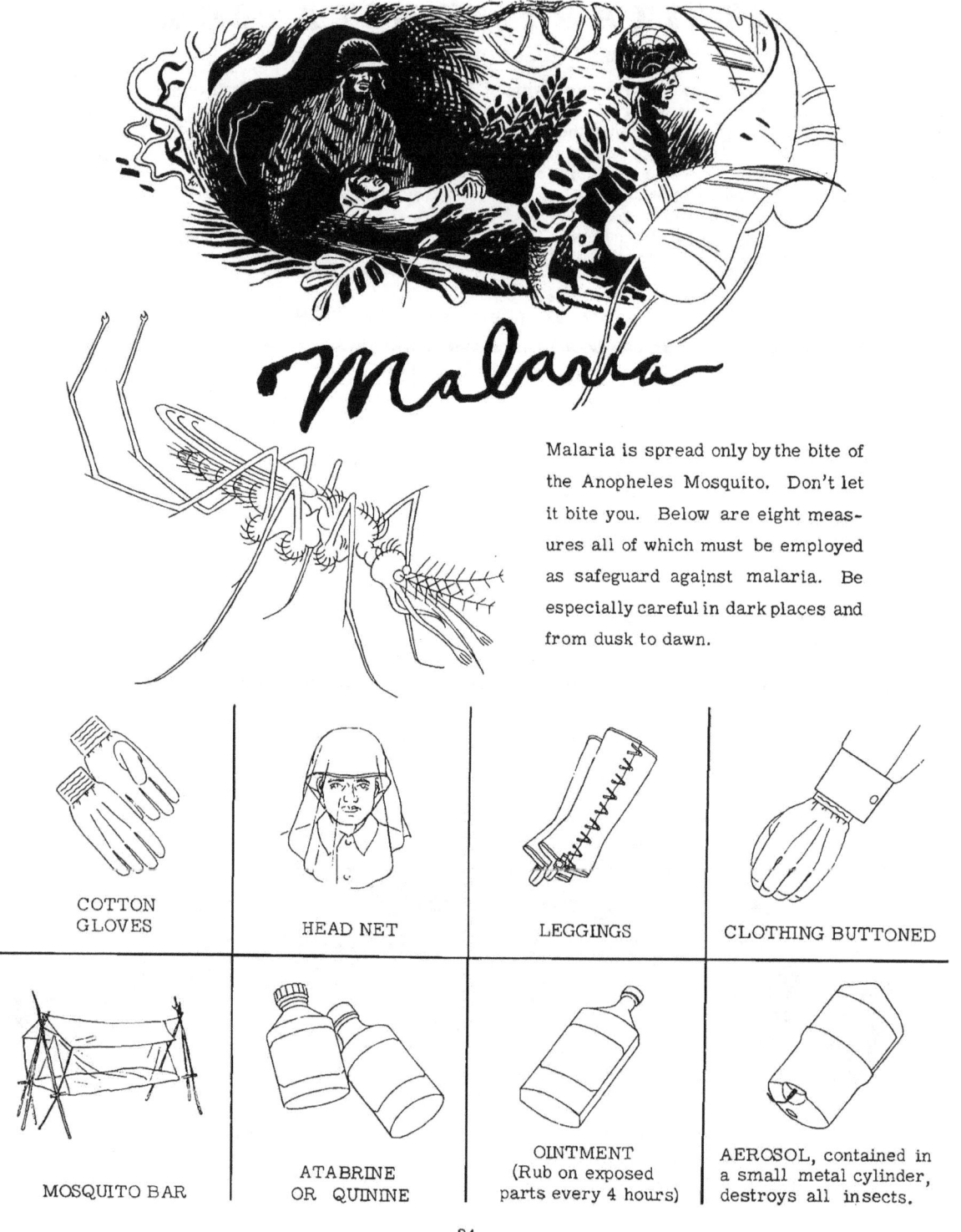

# Malaria

Malaria is spread only by the bite of the Anopheles Mosquito. Don't let it bite you. Below are eight measures all of which must be employed as safeguard against malaria. Be especially careful in dark places and from dusk to dawn.

| COTTON GLOVES | HEAD NET | LEGGINGS | CLOTHING BUTTONED |
|---|---|---|---|
| MOSQUITO BAR | ATABRINE OR QUININE | OINTMENT (Rub on exposed parts every 4 hours) | AEROSOL, contained in a small metal cylinder, destroys all insects. |

# Danger

HABITAT:_____

DISEASE:_____

TREATMENT:_____

_____

_____

HOUSE FLY

POISON OAK

POISON IVY

HABITAT:_____

DISEASE:_____

TREATMENT:_____

_____

_____

CRAB LOUSE

POISON SWAMP SUMAC

HABITAT:_____

DISEASE:_____

TREATMENT:_____

_____

_____

BED BUG

SYMPTOMS:_____

_____

_____

TREATMENT:_____

_____

_____

HABITAT:_____

DISEASE:_____

TREATMENT:_____

_____

_____

WOOD TICK

DELOUSING METHODS

1._____

2._____

3._____

HABITAT:_____

DISEASE:_____

TREATMENT:_____

_____

_____

BODY LOUSE

4._____

5._____

6._____

7._____

# FIRST AID

1. USE AVAILABLE MATERIAL - First aid packet, rifle, bayonet, belt, etc.
2. KEEP COOL - Don't get excited. It may cost a life.
3. STOP BLEEDING IMMEDIATELY - Patient can die in 5 minutes from loss of blood.
4. DON'T MOVE PATIENT - Until nature and extent of injuries are known.
5. KEEP PATIENT WARM - Cover patient with blankets. Treat for shock.

## WOUNDS

### 1. CONTROL OF BLEEDING

ELEVATION: ___

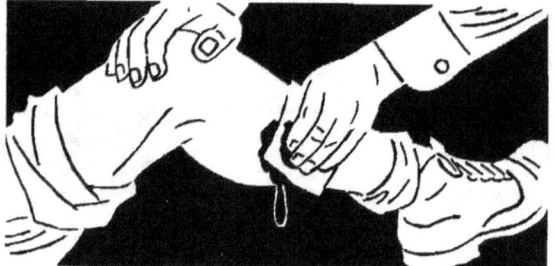

DIRECT PRESSURE: ___

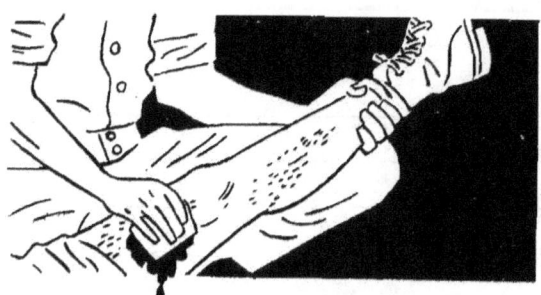

DIRECT PRESSURE AND ELEVATION: ___

TOURNIQUET: ___

# WOUNDS (cont'd)
## 2. PREVENT INFECTION

A. _____

B. _____

## 3. EASE SHOCK

SYMPTOMS: Chills, rapid weak pulse, vomiting, dazed pale appearance.

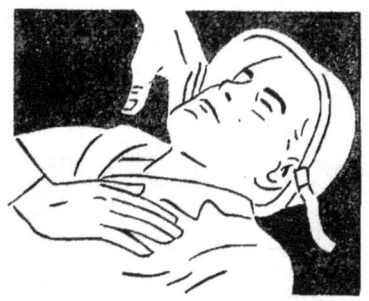

A. _____
_____

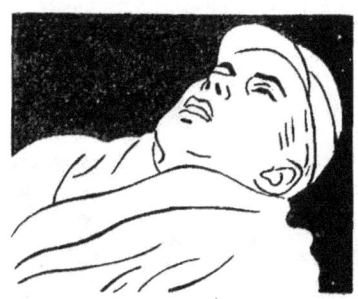

B. _____
_____

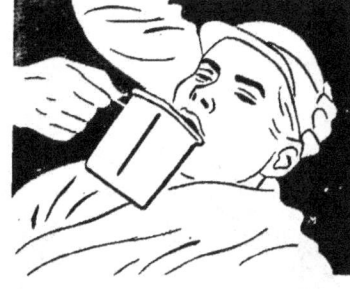

C. _____
_____

---

### FROSTBITE
Symptoms: Affected part is numb or painful. The color of the skin is not natural, being white or bluish-white. Treatment: Slowly thaw affected part. Do not rub or apply anything, such as snow or ice, that is colder than the part of the body affected.

### HEAT STROKE (Sun Stroke)
Symptoms: Flushed face, hot dry skin, rapid pulse, patient usually unconcious.
Treatment: Move the patient to a cool shaded place, loosen or remove clothing. Cool the patient gradually but GIVE NO STIMULANTS.

### HEAT EXHAUSTION
Symptoms: Pale face, rapid weak pulse, cold clammy skin, chills, staggering gait.
Treatment: Lie patient down with head low; allow patient to rest and give salt solution.

### SNAKE-BITE
Symptoms: Fang marks, pain, and swelling.
Treatment: Begin immediately! Have the patient rest, apply a tourniquet, and make the wound bleed by cutting cross incisions one-half inch wide over fang marks and at least one-fourth inch deep. Apply suction by means of mouth or heated bottles.

# FRACTURES

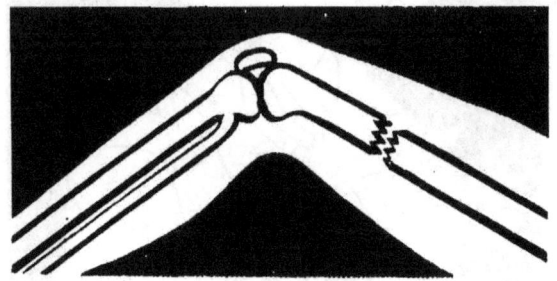

SIMPLE

SYMPTOMS _____

TREATMENT: Do not splint unless the patient must be moved. Treat for shock.

COMPOUND

SYMPTOMS: _____

TREATMENT: Control bleeding, prevent infection, treat for shock, and if necessary apply splints.

# SPLINTS

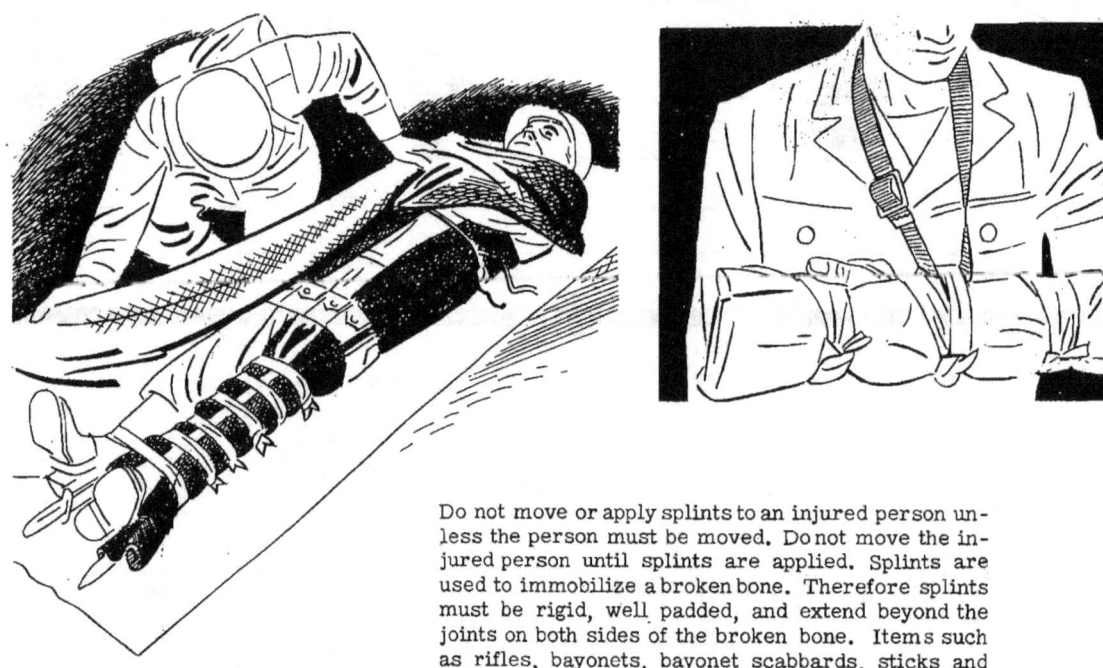

Do not move or apply splints to an injured person unless the person must be moved. Do not move the injured person until splints are applied. Splints are used to immobilize a broken bone. Therefore splints must be rigid, well padded, and extend beyond the joints on both sides of the broken bone. Items such as rifles, bayonets, bayonet scabbards, sticks and twigs, and even newspaper will make ideal splints.

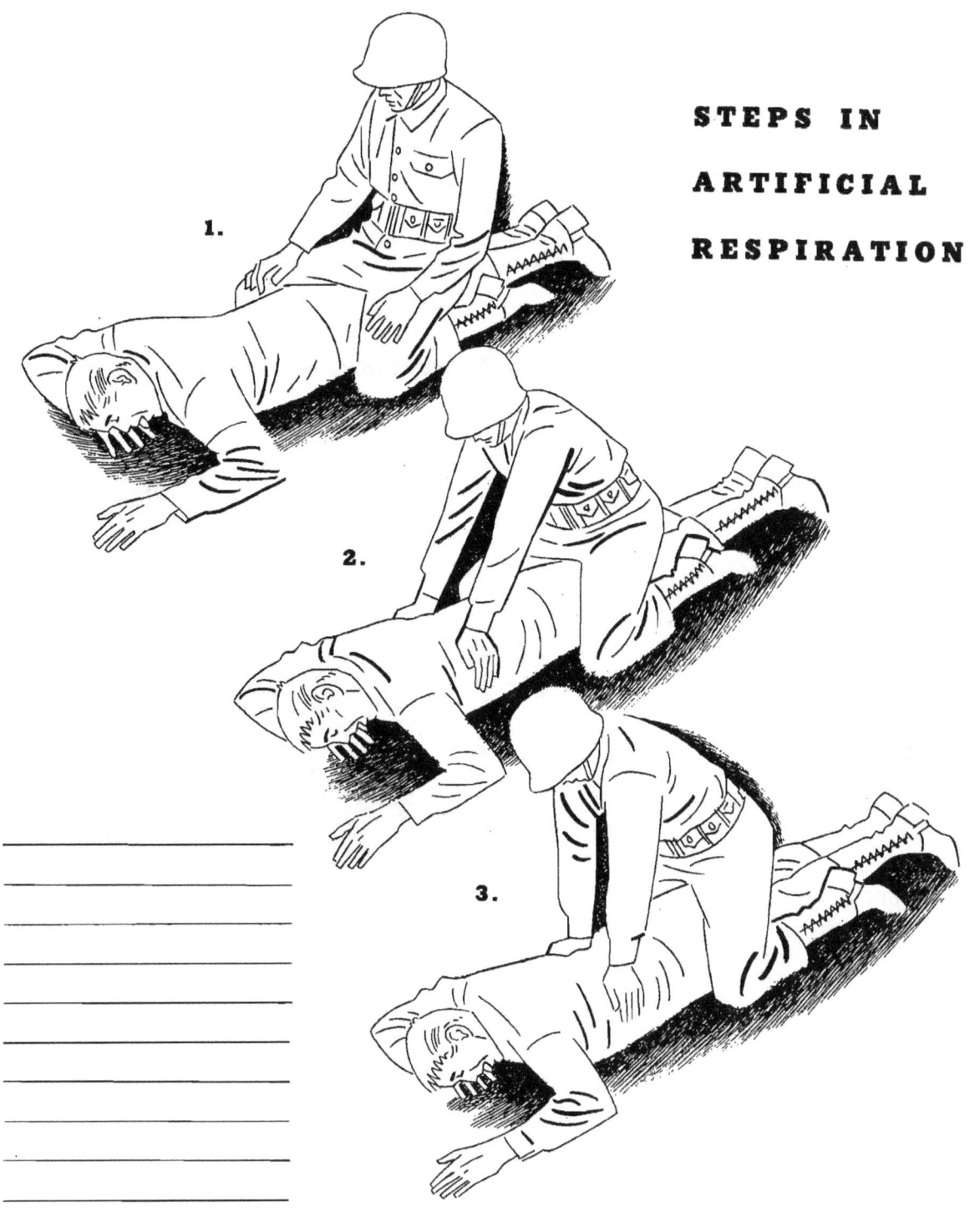

STEPS IN ARTIFICIAL RESPIRATION

# BURNS

| | APPEARANCE | TREATMENT |
|---|---|---|
| FIRST DEGREE | | |
| SECOND DEGREE | | |
| THIRD DEGREE | | |

IF WOUNDED IN COMBAT, THESE ARE MY LAWS OF

# SELF-AID

1. KEEP CALM

2. BARE THE WOUND

3. STOP THE BLEEDING

4. OPEN FIRST AID PACKET

5. SPRINKLE WOUND POWDER ON THE WOUND

6. APPLY THE BANDAGE

7. TAKE TWO "WOUND PILLS" IMMEDIATELY

8. LOOSEN TOURNIQUET OR CONSTRICTING BANDAGE EVERY 15 MINUTES

9. LIE DOWN BEHIND COVER AND KEEP AS WARM AS POSSIBLE UNTIL HELP COMES

10. TAKE ADDITIONAL "WOUND PILLS" (SEE BOX FOR DIRECTIONS)

# DEFENSE AGAINST CHEMICAL ATTACK

| CHEMICAL AGENTS | | | | | |
|---|---|---|---|---|---|
| COMMON NAMES | CW SYMBOL | PHYSICAL STATE | PERSISTENCY | TACTICAL USE | PHYSICAL EFFECT |
| Chlorine | Cl | Gas | Non-persistent | Casualty | Choking Gas |
| Phosgene | | | | | |
| Chlorpicrin | | | | | |
| Mustard | | | | | |
| Lewisite | | | | | |
| Adamsite | | | | | |
| Chloracetophenone | | | | | |
| Hexachlorethane | | | | | |
| White Phosphorus | | | | | |
| Thermit | | | ✕ | | |
| Magnesium | | | ✕ | | |

## INCENDIARY BOMBS

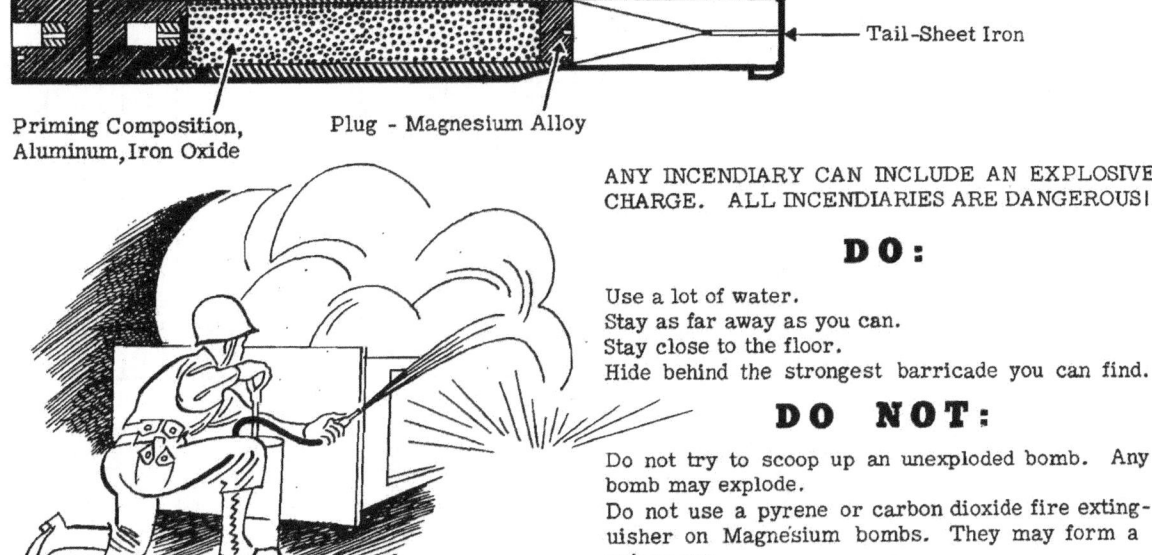

Priming Composition, Aluminum, Iron Oxide — Plug - Magnesium Alloy — Tail-Sheet Iron

ANY INCENDIARY CAN INCLUDE AN EXPLOSIVE CHARGE. ALL INCENDIARIES ARE DANGEROUS!

### DO:

Use a lot of water.
Stay as far away as you can.
Stay close to the floor.
Hide behind the strongest barricade you can find.

### DO NOT:

Do not try to scoop up an unexploded bomb. Any bomb may explode.
Do not use a pyrene or carbon dioxide fire extinguisher on Magnesium bombs. They may form a poison gas.

## PRINCIPAL CHEMICAL AGENTS

| PROPERTIES | COMMON NAME | CW SYMBOL | ODOR IN AIR | EFFECT ON BODY | CASUALTY DEVELOPS | FIRST AID |
|---|---|---|---|---|---|---|
| BLISTER GAS (VESICANT) | Mustard | H | Garlic, horseradish | Burns skin and lung tissue, temporary blindness | 4 to 24 Hours | * Warmth, quiet; apply, then remove, ointment; wash. Wash eyes with boric acid. |
| | Lewisite | L | Geraniums (sometimes burnt rubber) | Burns skin and lung tissue; causes arsenic poisoning and temporary blindness. | 30 min. | * Warmth, quiet; apply, then remove ointment; wash; apply hydrogen peroxide. |
| CHOKING GAS (LUNG IRRITANT) | Chlorine | Cl | Pungent | Irritates nose and throat; causes immediate choking. | At Once | * Keep quiet and warm; DO NOT EXERCISE. |
| | Phosgene | CG | Fresh cut hay; corn | Causes coughing; irritates eyes, nose, and throat, lung edema (water in lungs). | At Once or Delayed | * Keep quiet and warm; give tea or coffee. NO ALCOHOL. DO NOT EXERCISE. |
| | Chlorpicrin | PS | Sickening sweet; flypaper | Makes eyes water; causes vomiting. Irritates nose, throat and lungs. | At Once to 4 hours | * Keep quiet and warm; give light stimulants; DO NOT EXERCISE. |
| VOMITING GASES | Adamsite | DM | No odor yellow cloud | Sneezing; vomiting; headache; mentally depressing. | 5 to 10 minutes | * Breathe chlorine from weak solution of bleaching powder. |
| TEAR GAS (LACRIMATOR) | Chlor-acetophenone | CN | Apple blossoms | Eye and skin irritation. | At Once | * Face wind in pure air; wash eyes with boric acid. |
| SCREENING SMOKE | White Phosphorus | WP | Wet matches | Smoke — none. Particles cause flesh burns. | At Once | Keep wet; apply 5% copper sulfate solution, moist earth; wash with hot water. |
| | Hexa-chlorethane | HC | Sweet, astringent | None | None | Not necessary. |
| INCENDIARY | White Phosphorus | WP | | Flesh burns | At Once | WP as above; treat as ordinary heat or fire burns. |
| | Thermit | Th | | | | |
| | Magnesium | Mg | | | | |

* Mask patient in gassed area.

# PROTECTION FROM BLISTER GAS

You wear this EYESHIELD when a gas attack is expected to come. It protects your eyes until you get your mask on.

This WOOL HOOD is buttoned to your shirt and hangs down your back. It covers ears, neck, and head after your mask is on.

Wear LEGGINGS and GLOVES.

SOCKS, UNDERWEAR, and COVERALLS are dipped in chemicals which impregnate the clothes to make them gas proof.

SHOE IMPREGNITE is rubbed into your shoes to keep the leather from soaking up gas.

If you prepare in advance, you are protected in an attack.
BE PREPARED.

## DECONTAMINATION

To destroy gas on ground or on equipment, chloride of lime mixed with earth or water is used. For parts that would be hurt by rust or pitting, Non-Corrosive Decontamination Agent is used. Steam or water will destroy gas on clothes.

# AT THE COMMAND:
## "BY THE NUMBERS

Place rifle between the knees and remove the headpiece.

Hang helmet from left arm and quickly open carrier flap.

Withdraw mask and flip out head harness.

Grasp facepiece firmly. Raise it to a high chin position, with the chin well forward.

**2.** Thrust chin into mask. Pull straps over and check each one.

Seat mask to the face, by rubbing upward and backward along sides of facepiece.

**3.** Clear facepiece quickly by stopping outlet valve with palm of hand, blowing out vigorously.

Check mask by squeezing hose and breathing in. If mask adjustment is correct, facepiece should collapse against face.

**4.** Replace headpiece. Button carrier flap.

# AT THE COMMAND:
## "REMOVE AND REPLACE MASK"

TEST FOR GAS. Fill the lungs with air. Keep equipment off the ground. Open facepiece only to sniff. Clear the mask.

Remove headpiece. Pull facepiece forward, upward, and off. Hang mask over left arm. Replace helmet.

Replace in carrier, folding head harness in facepiece. Curl hose into facepiece. Rotate the assembly into carrier. Button carrier flap using rear snap.

## HOW TO SLING THE MASK:

  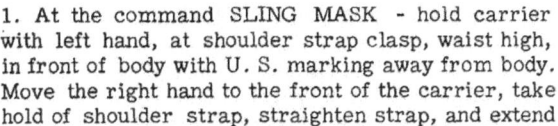

1. At the command SLING MASK - hold carrier with left hand, at shoulder strap clasp, waist high, in front of body with U. S. marking away from body. Move the right hand to the front of the carrier, take hold of shoulder strap, straighten strap, and extend to the right. (Fig. 1.)
2. Extend left arm to the left following with right arm. Pass shoulder strap over left hand and elbow, over the head, over right shoulder, and engage the clasp. Fasten the body strap. (Figs. 2 and 3.)

### WHEN TO TEST FOR GAS:

1. As soon as your mask is on, unless you already know what kind of gas it is.
2. Always, before removing the mask

### HOW TO TEST FOR GAS:

Fill lungs with air. Get down close to ground. Keep equipment off the ground. Open facepiece to sniff. Clear the facepiece immediately.

### REMEMBER:

AT THE COMMAND "GAS!" WITHOUT THE NUMBERS
WHEN THE GAS ALARM IS SOUNDED...
WHEN YOU SMELL GAS...
WHEN YOU EVEN SUSPECT GAS...

**STOP BREATHING AND PUT ON YOUR GAS MASK AS FAST AS YOU CAN**

# HASTY FIELD FORTIFICATIONS

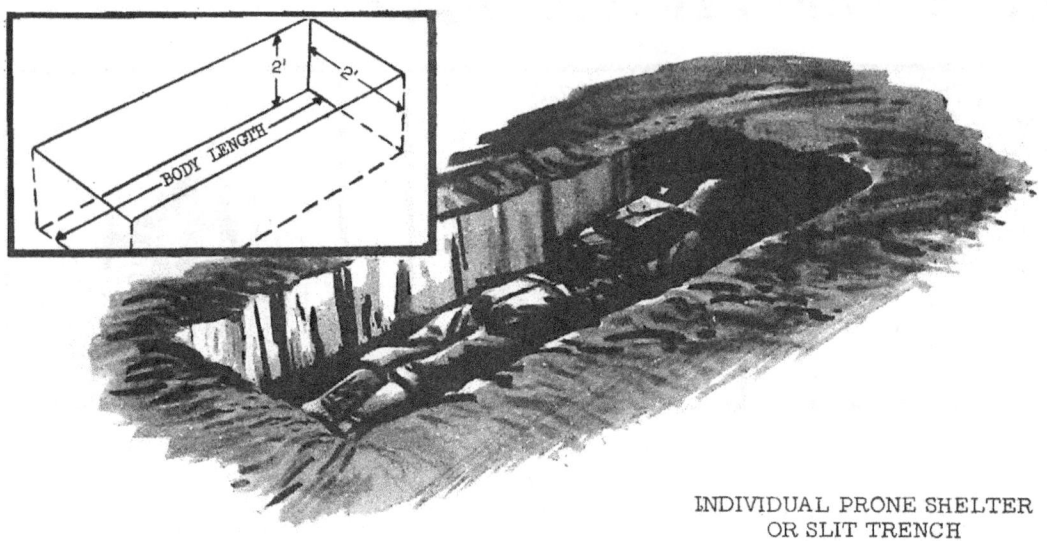

### INDIVIDUAL PRONE SHELTER OR SLIT TRENCH

When a halt is for more than a few minutes (but less than 6 hours), such as a halt in an assembly area, individual prone shelters are constructed. Full advantage is taken of natural cover and concealment in locating these shelters. This entrenchment can be dug quickly and allows the individual to obtain rest and protection simultaneously. It furnishes protection from airplane strafing and bombs, artillery fragments (except time-fire) and small-arms fire, but is not protection against the crushing effect of a tank.

If it becomes necessary to remain in the area for a greater length of time than 6 hours, the slit trench can readily be converted into a two man foxhole.

### STANDING TYPE FOXHOLES

When a halt is made for more than six hours, standing type, one or two man fox holes are dug. These will protect you against bomb or shell fragments (except time-fire) and small-arms fire. The fox hole should be dug sufficiently deep to allow a clearance of two or more feet between the ground surface and the highest part of your body when crouched in the bottom. This will provide protection against the crushing effect of tanks.

The corners of the fox hole should be rounded to minimize shadows. Good camouflage can be effected by improvising a cover made from garnished chicken wire or interlaced branches matching the terrain.

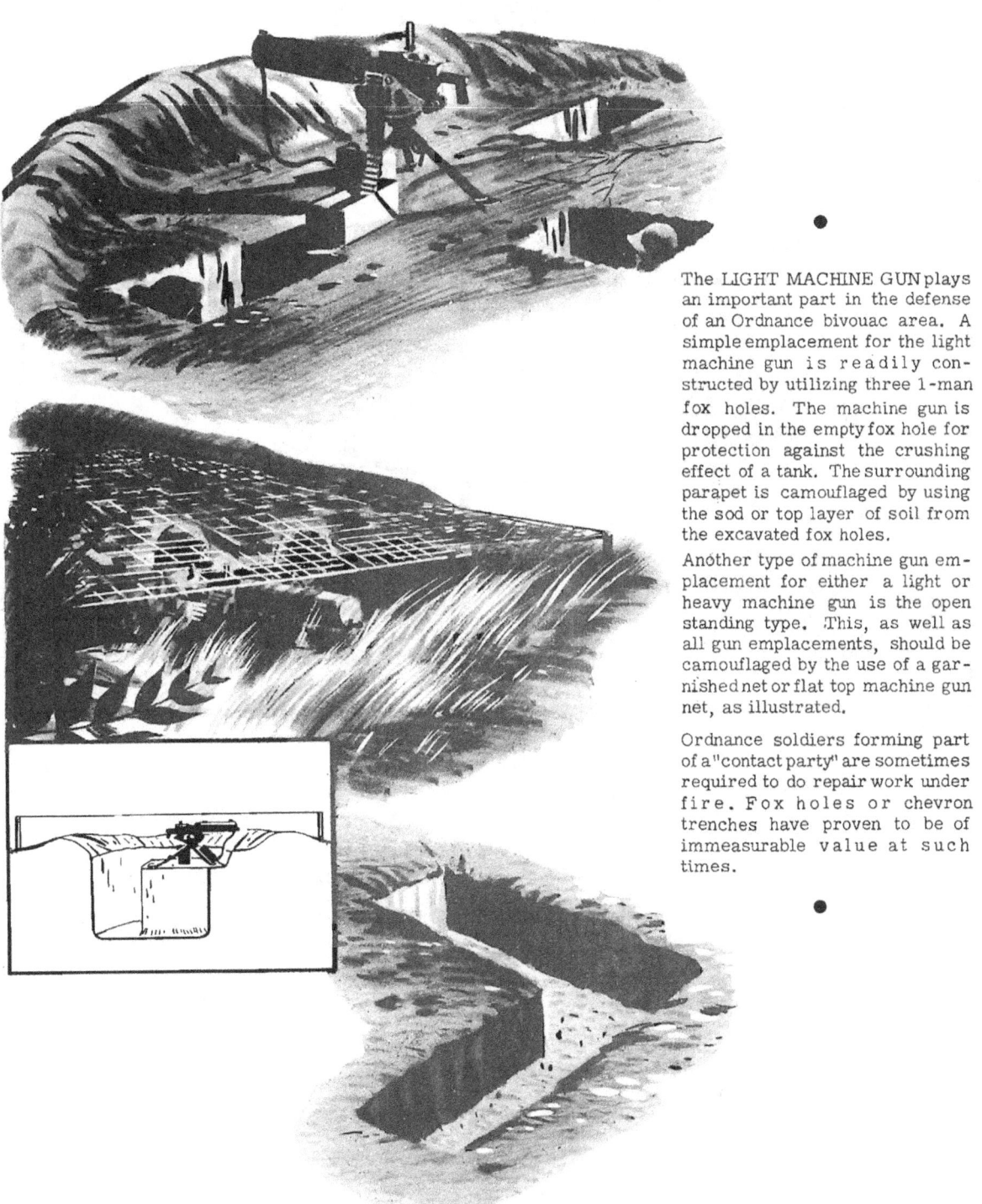

The LIGHT MACHINE GUN plays an important part in the defense of an Ordnance bivouac area. A simple emplacement for the light machine gun is readily constructed by utilizing three 1-man fox holes. The machine gun is dropped in the empty fox hole for protection against the crushing effect of a tank. The surrounding parapet is camouflaged by using the sod or top layer of soil from the excavated fox holes.

Another type of machine gun emplacement for either a light or heavy machine gun is the open standing type. This, as well as all gun emplacements, should be camouflaged by the use of a garnished net or flat top machine gun net, as illustrated.

Ordnance soldiers forming part of a "contact party" are sometimes required to do repair work under fire. Fox holes or chevron trenches have proven to be of immeasurable value at such times.

# CAMOUFLAGE

PURPOSE: 1. HIDING  2. BLENDING  3. DECEPTION

MEANS OF DETECTION: 1. AERIAL PHOTOGRAPHY  2. DIRECT OBSERVATION

## CAMOUFLAGE MATERIALS

### 1. NATURAL

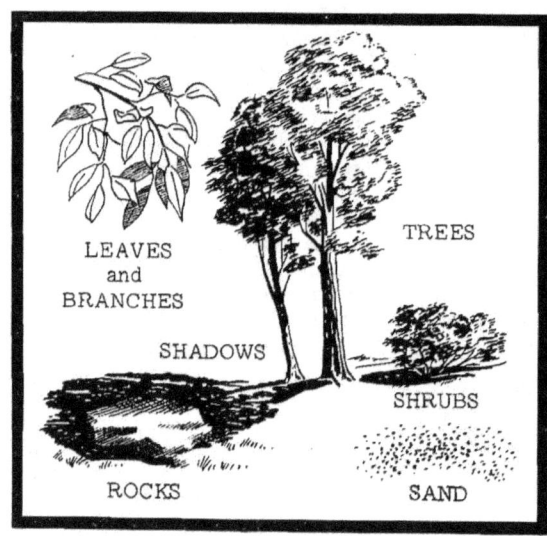

### 2. ARTIFICIAL

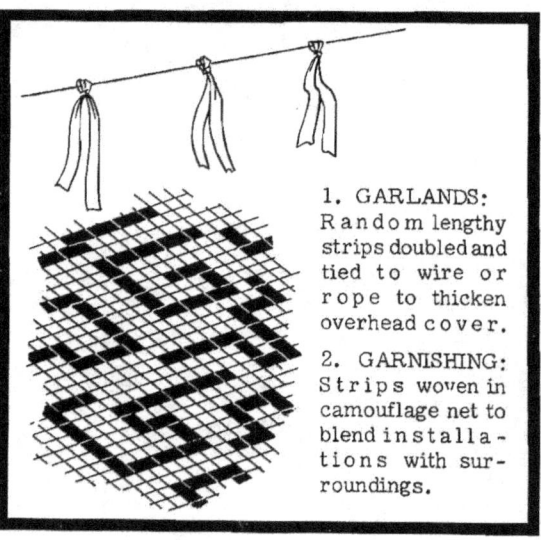

1. GARLANDS: Random lengthy strips doubled and tied to wire or rope to thicken overhead cover.

2. GARNISHING: Strips woven in camouflage net to blend installations with surroundings.

#### ADVANTAGES

1. Matches terrain very readily.
2. Easily procured.
3. Usually found in abundance.

#### DISADVANTAGES

1. Extreme care must be taken in selecting material to avoid changing appearance of terrain.
2. Must be changed regularly.
3. Care must be exercised when gathering material so as not to change appearance of area.

#### ADVANTAGES

1. Quite permanent in nature.
2. Requires less labor to maintain.
3. Very effective if used correctly.

#### DISADVANTAGES

1. Artificial materials are very bulky, consequently they present a transportation problem.
2. Considerably more care and skill are required to erect an installation of this type.

### REMEMBER:

1. Shadows of objects are generally more readily distinguished than the object.
2. Nothing photographs exactly like snow; however any white material is satisfactory for concealment from direct observation.

FLAT TOP (NATURAL MATERIALS)

Keep top flat. Place trees and shrubs vertically, tying to supporting wire. Make outline of complete installation irregular. Change natural material periodically.

FLAT TOP (ARTIFICIAL MATERIALS)

Garnishing must not be woven parallel to outer edge of net. Garnishing should cover approximately 75% of area at center and thinned to 15% at edge. Top must be flat and taut during day.

DRAPE

Garnished camouflage net must be staked and propped to distort natural outline of installation. Garnishing may be of only one color or several that blend to desired tone.

DECEPTION

Care must be taken not to make camouflage mistakes in dummy position too noticeable. Remember, the enemy is no fool. Dummy installation should be at least 1 mile from true position.

1. Make no changes visible from the air.

WRONG

RIGHT

2. Use natural cover and concealment when available.

WRONG

RIGHT

3. Match terrain pattern.

WRONG

RIGHT

4. Break up shadows.

WRONG

RIGHT

5. Choose proper location.

WRONG

RIGHT

6. Observe camouflage discipline.

WRONG

RIGHT

# CAMOUFLAGE UNIFORMS

Even though these uniforms may not be available to you, a bit of paint, waste material, and resourcefulness will enable you effectively to improvise them.

JUNGLE SUIT

RAGAMUFFIN SUIT

SNOW SUIT

## NOTES ON CAMOUFLAGE

_____     _____
_____     _____
_____     _____
_____     _____
_____     _____
_____     _____
_____     _____
_____     _____

**OBSERVE CAMOUFLAGE DISCIPLINE ...
CAMOUFLAGE DISCIPLINE IS YOUR RESPONSIBILITY**

# DEFENSE AGAINST MECHANIZED ATTACK

## IDENTIFICATION

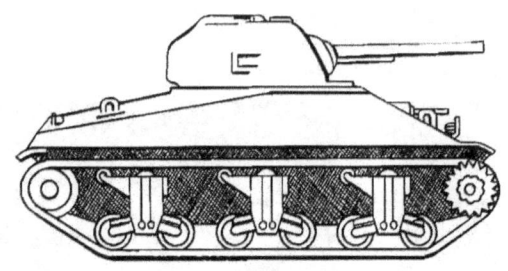

AMERICAN TANK; MEDIUM, M4A2

American Bogie Wheel Assembly

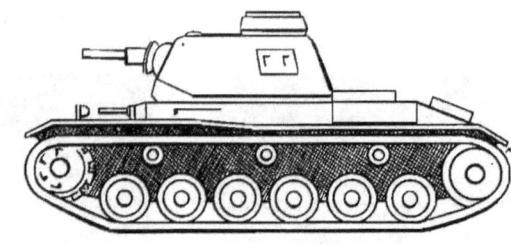

FOREIGN TANK

Bogie wheels may be in rows of even sized wheels or interlocking as at right below.

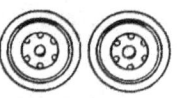 

| AMERICAN | | FOREIGN |
|---|---|---|
| | 1. BOGIE WHEELS: | |
| | 2. HULL: | |
| | 3. TURRET: | |
| | 4. SILHOUETTE: | |
| | 5. INSIGNIA: | |
| | 6. LOCATION OF ARMAMENT: | |
| | 7. TYPE OF ARMAMENT: | |

## VULNERABLE POINTS ON A TANK

## NATURAL TERRAIN OBSTACLES

A. _____    C. _____    E. _____
B. _____    D. _____    F. _____

## ARTIFICIAL BARRIERS

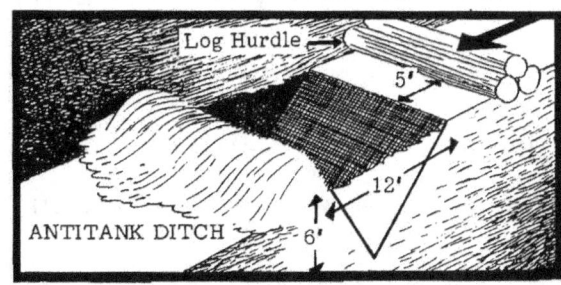
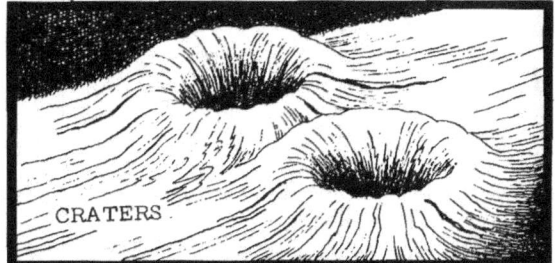

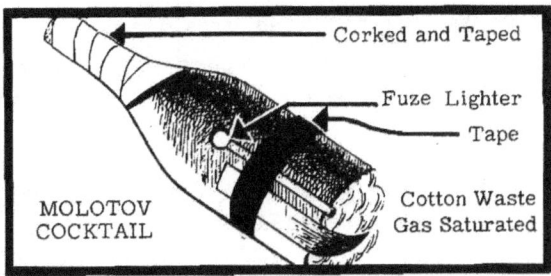
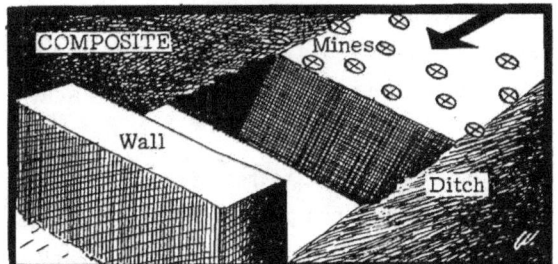

# MINES AND MINEFIELDS

The Ordnance Soldier may frequently be required to lay a hasty mine field, either to protect his bivouac area or to delay the enemy. The most efficient method for laying a hasty mine field is outlined below.

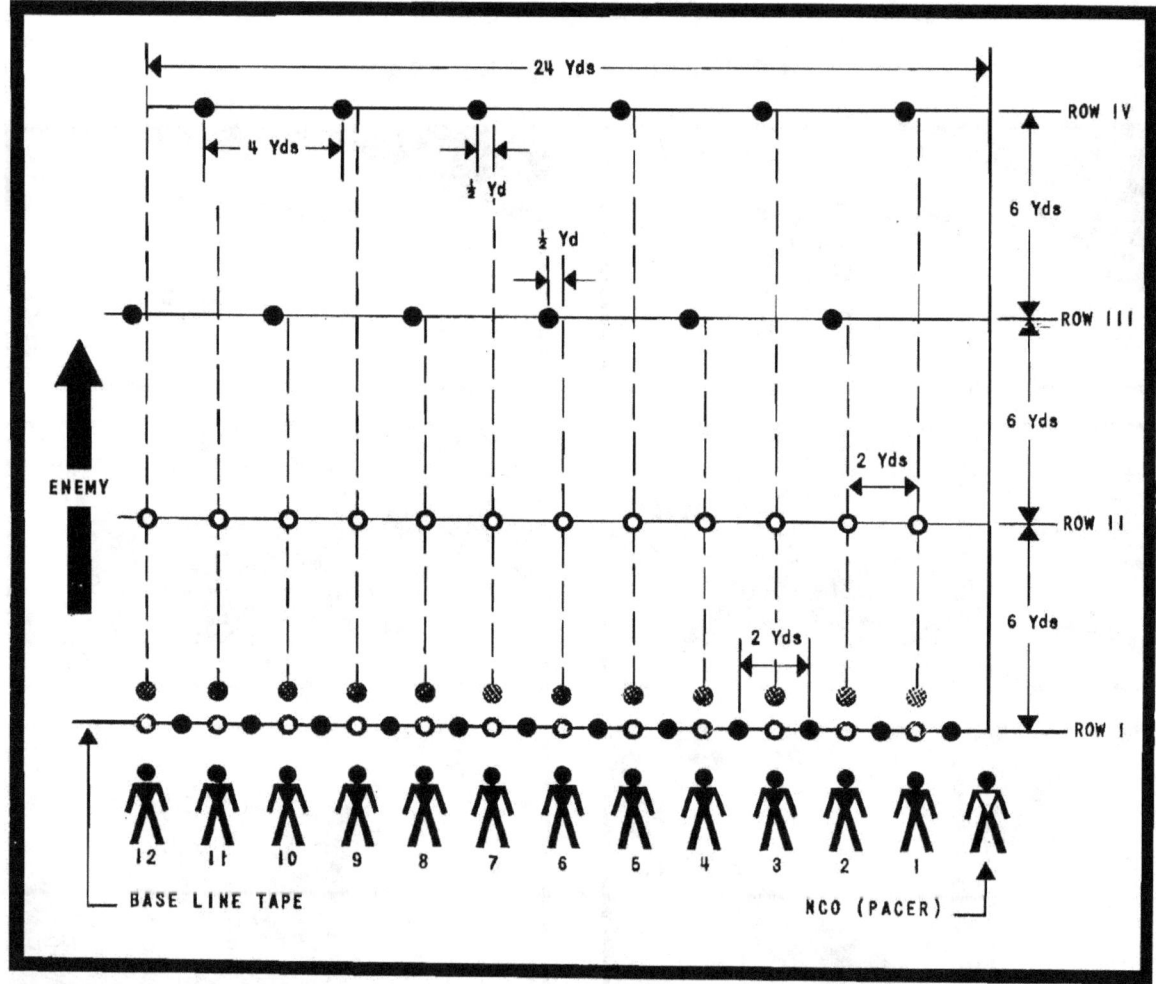

**1.** 36 mines are placed alternately single and double along base line tape at 1 yard intervals paced off by NCO in charge, the single mines FORMING ROW I.

**2.** Laying party lines up in front of double mines and at given signal each man picks up 2 mines and moves forward 6 yards to place one mine, FORMING ROW II.

**3.** The laying party then advances 6 yards farther, halts, and even numbered men place their remaining mine 1/2 yard to their left, FORMING ROW III.

**4.** On signal the laying party advances an additional 6 yards and odd numbered men place their remaining mine 1/2 yard to their left, FORMING ROW IV.

A mine field must be covered by fire power to be fully effective.

If an undefended mine field is left to delay the enemy, that delay is only as long as it takes the enemy to pass or clear a path through the minefield. To lengthen the delay, the hasty mine field is camouflaged with leaves, grass, or small branches.

# ANTITANK MINE

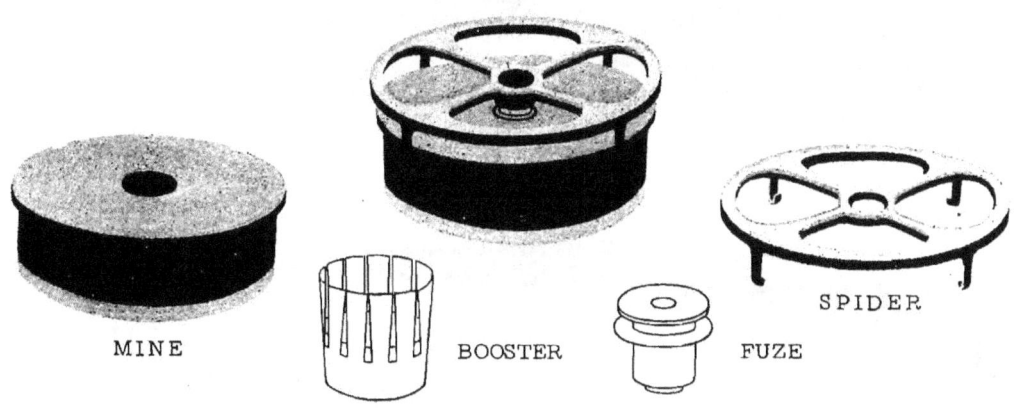

MINE    BOOSTER    FUZE    SPIDER

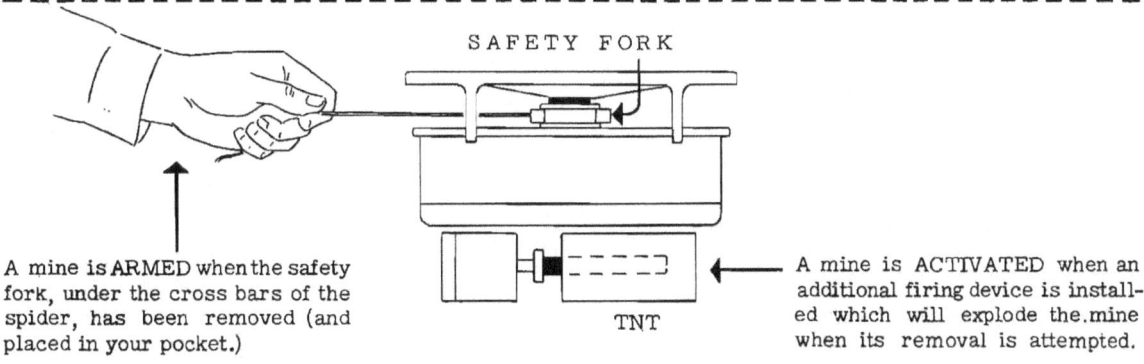

SAFETY FORK

TNT

A mine is ARMED when the safety fork, under the cross bars of the spider, has been removed (and placed in your pocket.)

A mine is ACTIVATED when an additional firing device is installed which will explode the mine when its removal is attempted.

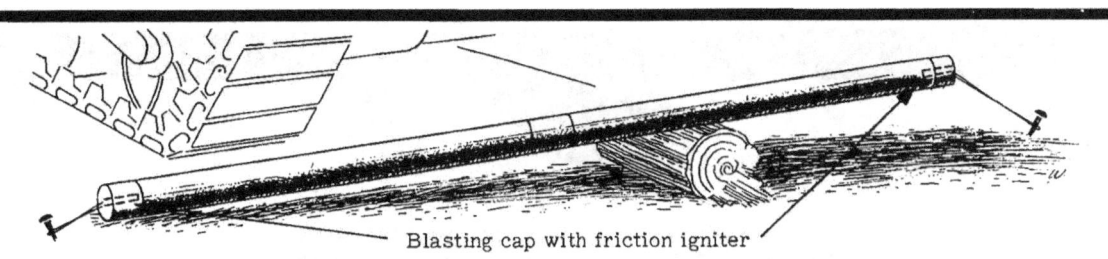

Blasting cap with friction igniter

BANGALORE TORPEDO USED AS AN ANTITANK MINE

# GRENADES

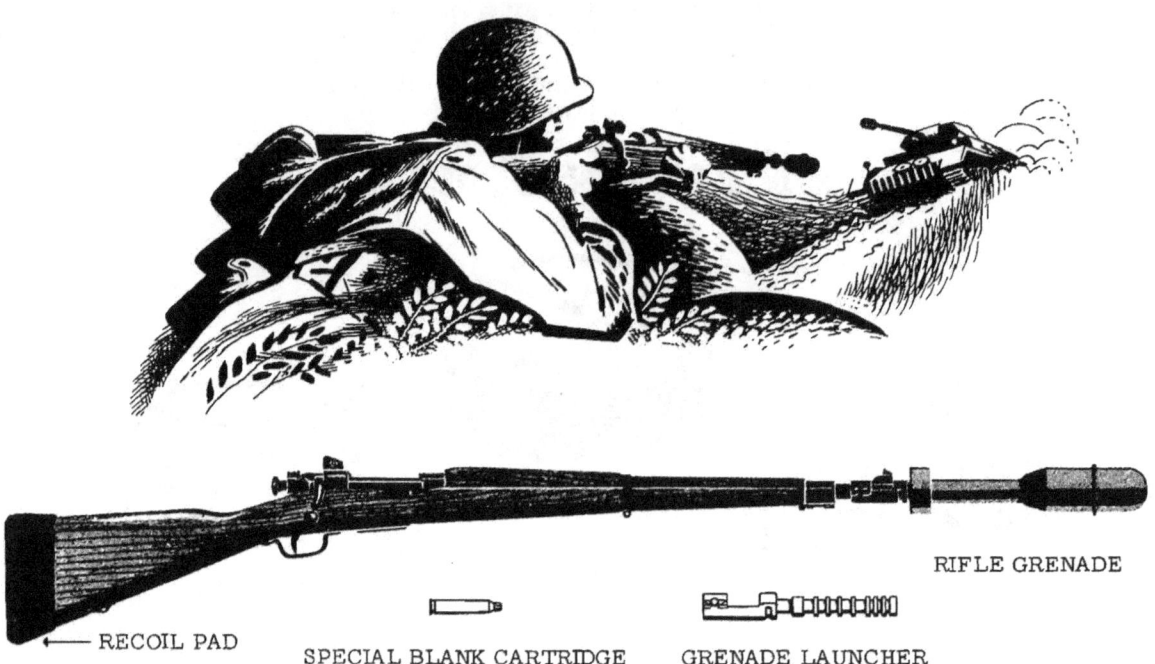

The Ordnance Soldier is required to have a knowledge of grenades not only because he may be responsible for their storage and issue, but because grenades have proven to be of inestimable defense value to Ordnance Soldiers in the combat zone.

The Antitank grenade contains a high explosive charge and is used principally against tanks and armored vehicles. It is fired by means of a launcher attached to the muzzle of the rifle or carbine.

A special type of blank cartridge is used to fire the grenade. No other will be used.

A rubber recoil pad protects the rifle stock when the rifle is fired with the butt resting against a hard surface. The pad also lessens the shock of recoil when firing is done from the shoulder.

Do not drop the grenade. Load close to the ground and keep the muzzle elevated.

The Antitank Rocket, M6 is a high explosive fired from the "Bazooka" and has proven very effective against enemy tanks. (See page 88 for detail drawing of rocket)

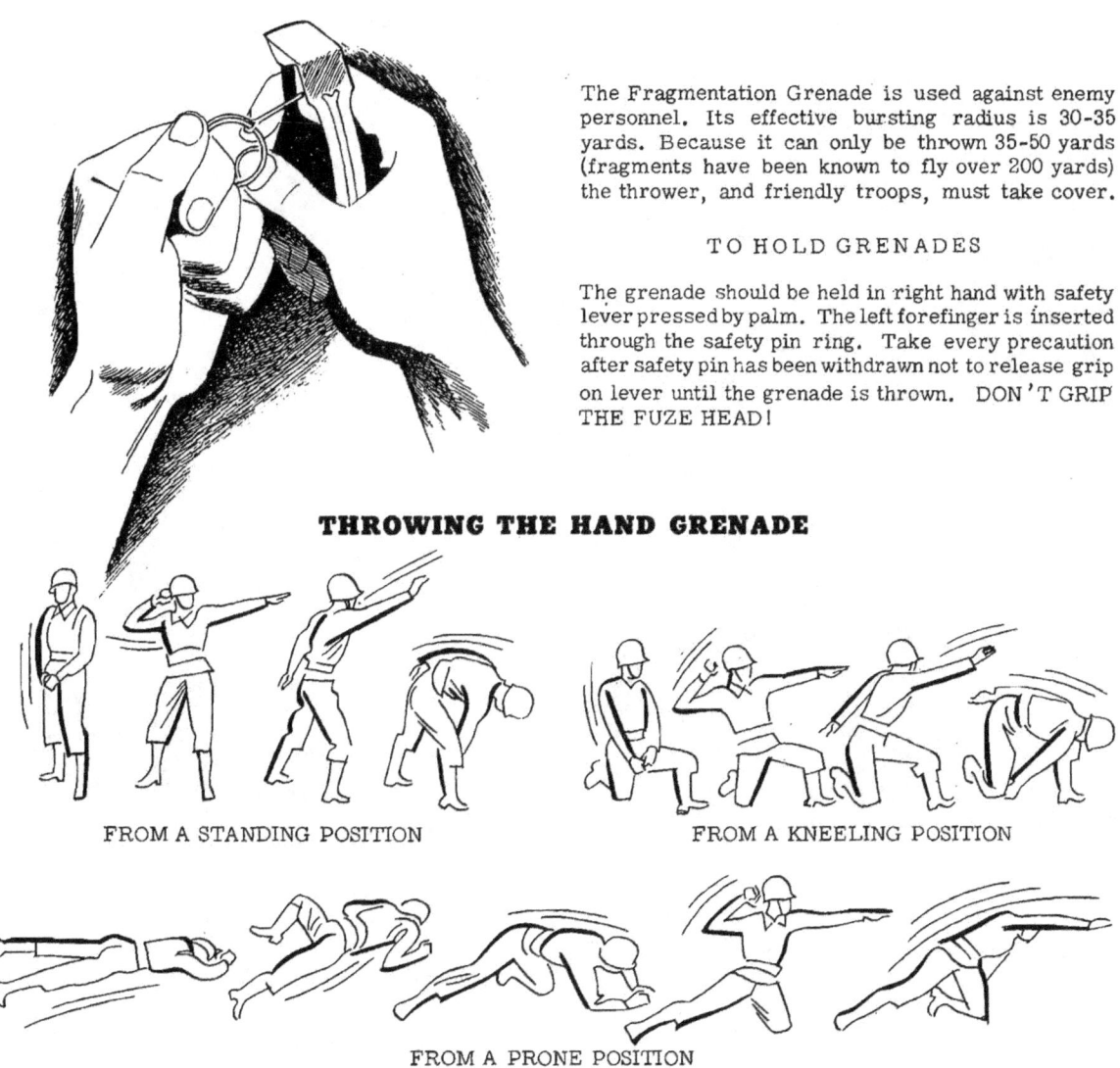

The Fragmentation Grenade is used against enemy personnel. Its effective bursting radius is 30-35 yards. Because it can only be thrown 35-50 yards (fragments have been known to fly over 200 yards) the thrower, and friendly troops, must take cover.

### TO HOLD GRENADES

The grenade should be held in right hand with safety lever pressed by palm. The left forefinger is inserted through the safety pin ring. Take every precaution after safety pin has been withdrawn not to release grip on lever until the grenade is thrown. DON'T GRIP THE FUZE HEAD!

## THROWING THE HAND GRENADE

FROM A STANDING POSITION

FROM A KNEELING POSITION

FROM A PRONE POSITION

Hand grenades include several types. They are shown in detail on page 84.

The Offensive Hand Grenade consists of TNT packed in a paper container and the same fuze assembly used in the Fragmentation Grenade. It is used mainly against obstacles and enemy installations.

The Chemical Hand Grenade consists of a gas or smoke filler packed in a perforated metal container and the same fuze assembly used in the Fragmentation Grenade. The perforations are covered by adhesive patches which are destroyed when the grenade is set off. It is used for signalling, creating smoke screens and for gas warfare.

The Frangible Hand Grenade, better known as the "Molotov Cocktail", can easily be improvised by filling a quart bottle with gasoline and sealing the cap. A cloth (or any absorbent material) soaked with gasoline is tied around the bottle. The cloth is ignited and the "cocktail" thrown at the target. (See page 43.)

When carrying hand grenades in your pocket make sure the safety pin ring is not sticking out of your pocket. A tree branch, or bush, or a practical joking Nazi or Jap, might pull it out..

# DEFENSE AGAINST AIR AND PARATROOP ATTACK

ON THE MARCH, You may get only a few seconds warning. Disperse laterally to both sides of the road running 10 to 50 paces depending upon your position in the squad. You are safest in a depression, but remember that ditches are systematically strafed. Each squad member should know in advance where he is to go, taking advantage of cover and concealment, especially shadows. Never attempt to escape by continued running, for the pilot probably has not seen you, but is sure to see you when you run.

IN A VEHICLE, drive to the side of the road, set brakes and run for cover. Don't get under the vehicle, the principal target. Take cover as on march.

IN BIVOUAC, dig a slit trench at the first opportunity. When attacked, get in it and remain motionless.

### POINTS TO REMEMBER ... PARATROOP ATTACK

1. _____
2. _____
3. _____

# IDENTIFICATION OF AIRCRAFT

### U. S. ARMY AIRCRAFT

PURSUITS, INTERCEPTORS

P38, Lockhead Lightning
P39, Bell Airacobra
P40, Curtiss Warhawk
P47, Republic Thunderbolt
P51, North American Mustang

LIGHT AND MEDIUM BOMBERS

A20, Douglas Boston
A25, Curtiss Helldiver
B18, Douglas Bolo
B25, North American Mitchell
B26, Martin Marauder

HEAVY BOMBERS

B17, Boeing Flying Fortress
B24, Consolidated Liberator

## WINGS

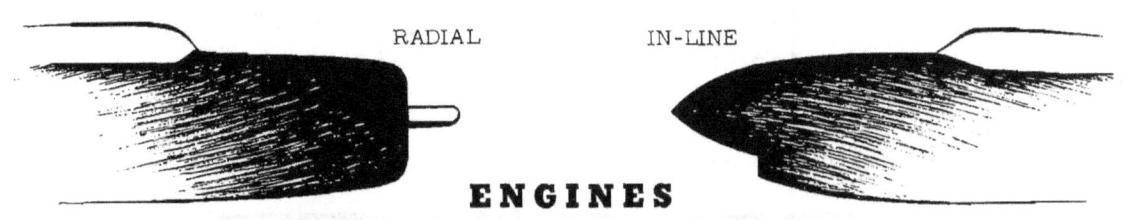

## ENGINES

## TAILS

## INSIGNIA

U.S.A.
White and Blue

RUSSIA
Red

BRITAIN
Red, White and Blue

GERMANY
Black

JAPAN
Red

# MAP READING

A map is a scale drawing of a portion of the earth's surface as seen from directly above. To read a map the soldier must be able to identify symbols, compute distances and determine directions.

## SYMBOLS

| MILITARY | | CONVENTIONAL |
|---|---|---|
| SQUAD _____ | ARMORED COMMAND _____ | BUILDING _____ |
| SECTION _____ | ARMY AIR FORCES _____ | FENCE, BARBED WIRE _____ |
| PLATOON _____ | ARTILLERY _____ | FENCE, SMOOTH WIRE _____ |
| COMPANY _____ | CAVALRY _____ | GRASSLAND _____ |
| BATTALION _____ | ENGINEERS _____ | RAILROAD _____ |
| REGIMENT _____ | INFANTRY _____ | ROAD, PRIMARY _____ |
| BRIGADE _____ | MEDICAL _____ | ROAD, SECONDARY _____ |
| DIVISION _____ | ORDNANCE _____ | SWAMP _____ |
| CORPS _____ | QUARTERMASTER _____ | TELEGRAPH POLES _____ |
| ARMY _____ | SIGNAL CORPS _____ | TREES, BROADLEAVED _____ |

## MAP SCALES

All scales are written statements of ratio (or relationship) between map distance and ground distance.

| TYPE OF SCALE | EXAMPLE | EXPLANATION |
|---|---|---|
| 1. Words and figures | 1" = 5000' | Map distance on left of equal sign; ground distance on right of equal sign. |
| 2. Graphic | 1000 500 0 1000 | Primary scale to right of 0; extension to left of 0. |
| 3. Representative Fraction | $\frac{1}{62500}$ | Top figure is always 1. Top and bottom figures express identical units. |

# DIRECTION

### TO USE A MAP WE MUST BE ABLE TO DETERMINE DIRECTION

**1.**
Direction is always measured from a type of North

TRUE NORTH is found by _____

MAGNETIC NORTH is found by _____

GRID NORTH is found by _____

SYMBOLS:

**2.**
Direction of a line is indicated by:

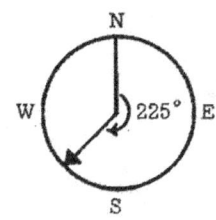

AZIMUTH...angle measured clockwise from some type of north. Maximum Azimuth is 360 degrees.

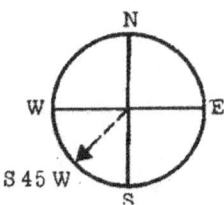

BEARING...angle measured from North or South to East or West to a maximum of 90°

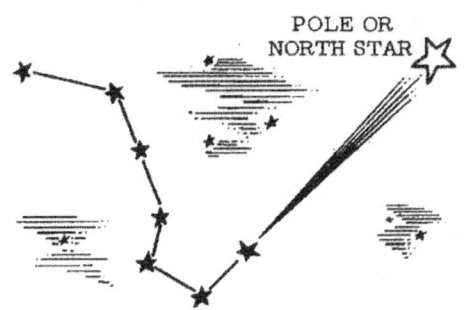

### TRUE NORTH BY NORTH STAR (POLARIS)

Method: Two pointer stars form line approaching North Star which is brightest star in vicinity. Line dropped from North Star to ground locates true North.

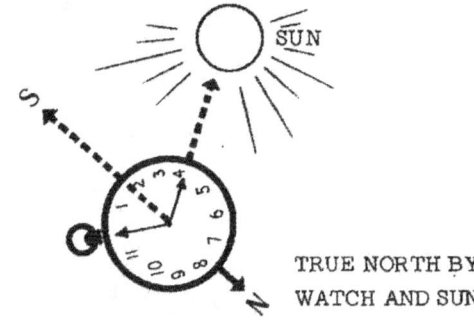

### TRUE NORTH BY WATCH AND SUN

Method: Point hour hand in direction of sun. Half way between hour hand and 12 is true south. Opposite direction, true North.

Limitations: 1. Watch must give correct sun time.
2. Very inaccurate near noon and near equator.
3. Take smallest angle between hour hand and 12.
4. Use method only between 0600 and 1800.

# COMPASSES

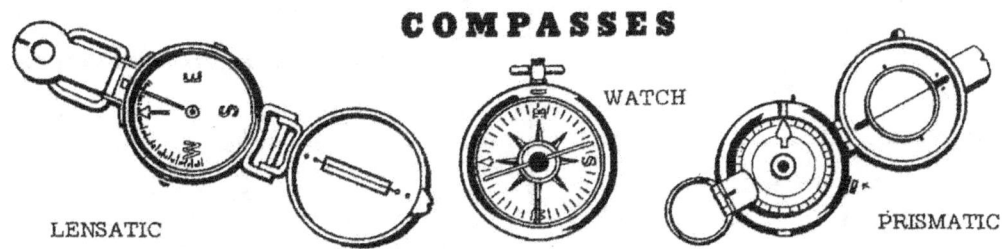

LENSATIC     WATCH     PRISMATIC

# ORIENTING A MAP

Turn map so points on map are in same position in relation to observer as points on ground.

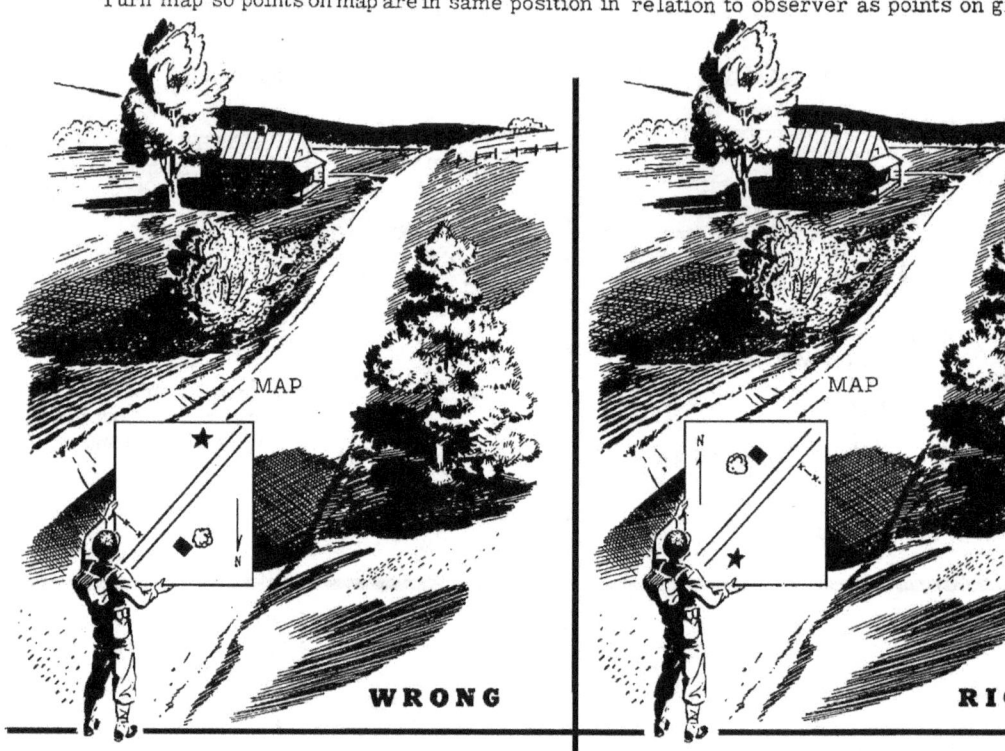

WRONG

RIGHT

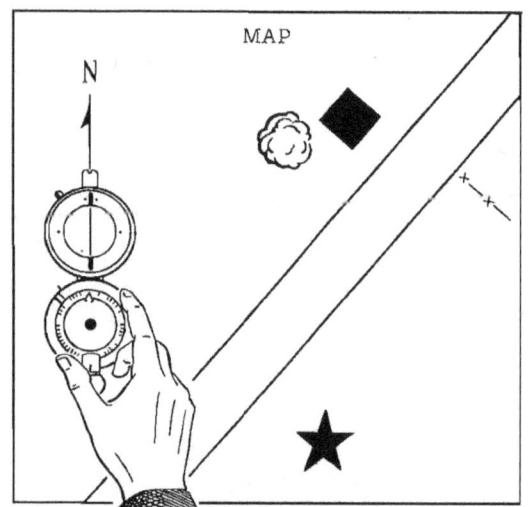

ORIENTING A MAP WITH COMPASS

Place Magnetic North line on map in alignment with needle of Compass.

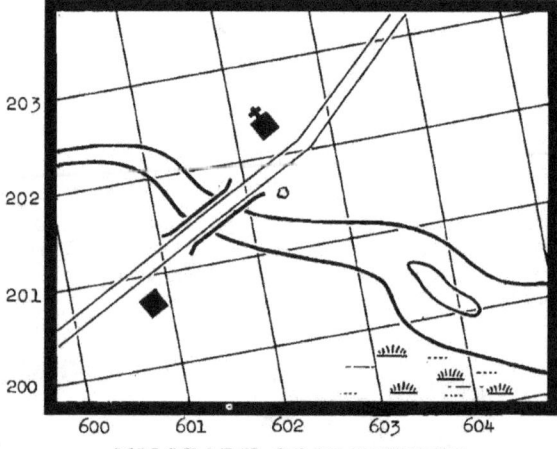

MILITARY GRID SYSTEM

The Military Grid System is primarily used to locate points on map and aid in relaying this information in messages. To use Military Grid System the rule "Read Right Up" must be remembered. Locate object at 602.4 — 201.6

(ABOVE)
OVERHEAD PICTURE
OF GROUND

# CONTOUR LINES

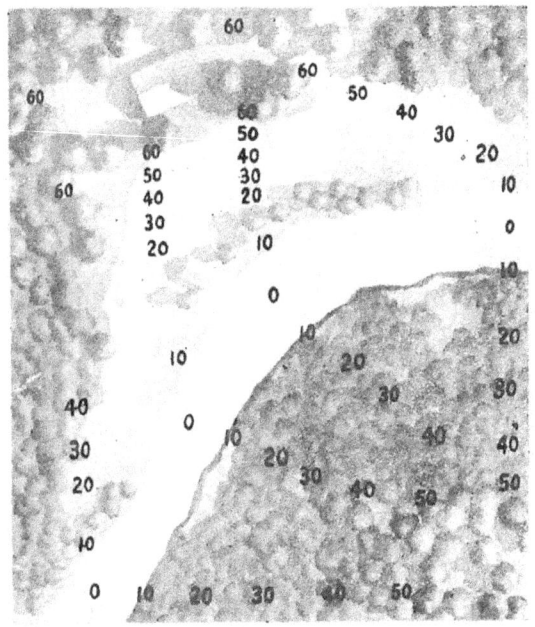

(ABOVE)
ELEVATION OF
POINTS ON GROUND

Contour lines are drawn on a map to indicate the different elevations on the land surfaces.

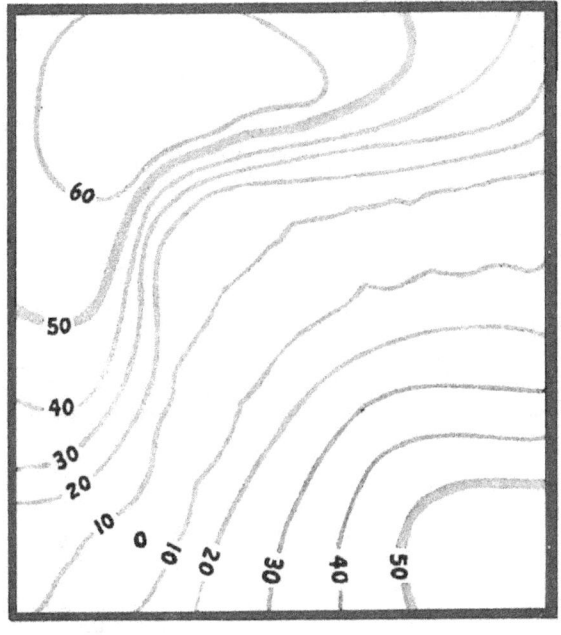

(AT LEFT)
GROUND REPRESENTED
BY CONTOUR LINES

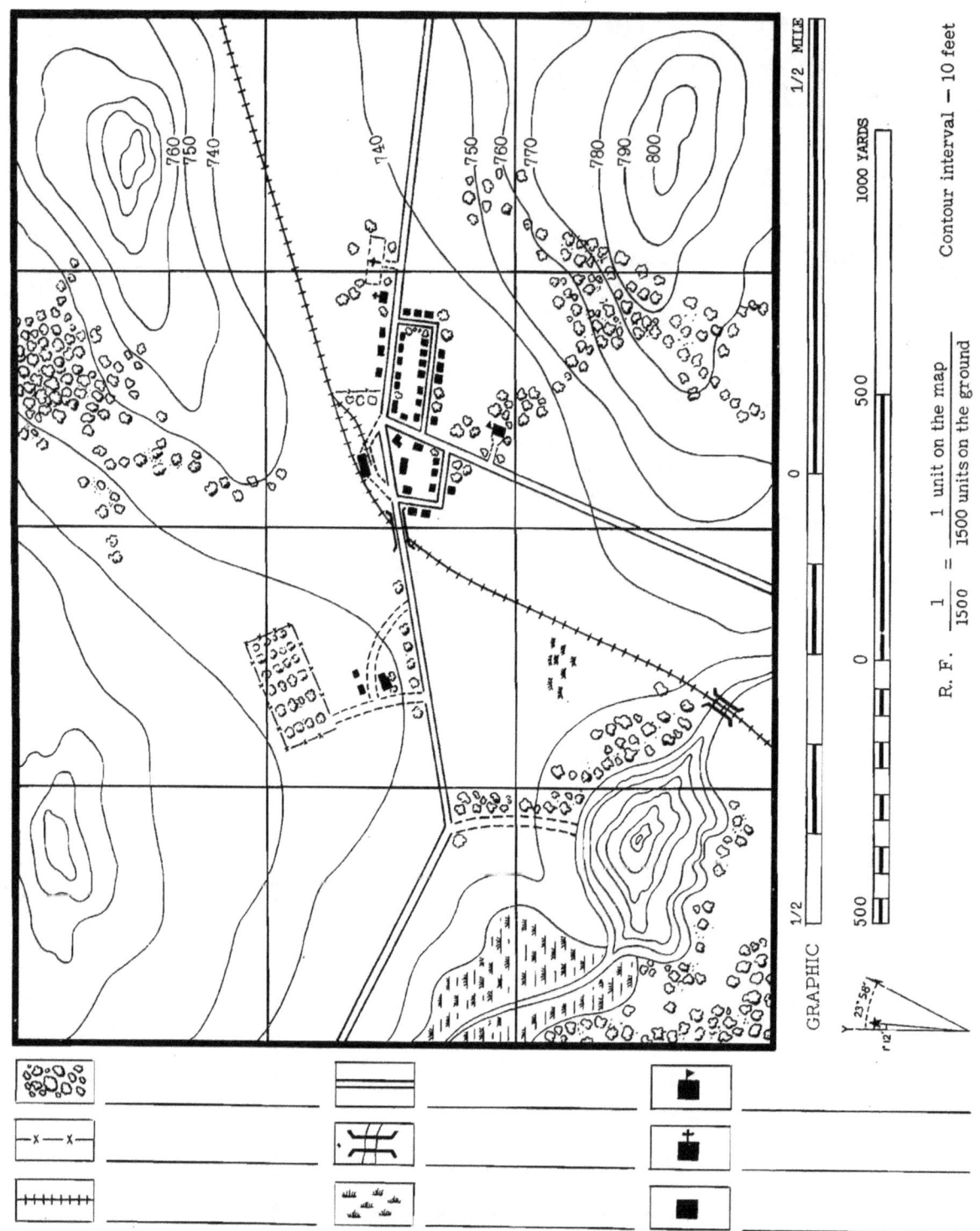

# KNOTS AND HITCHES

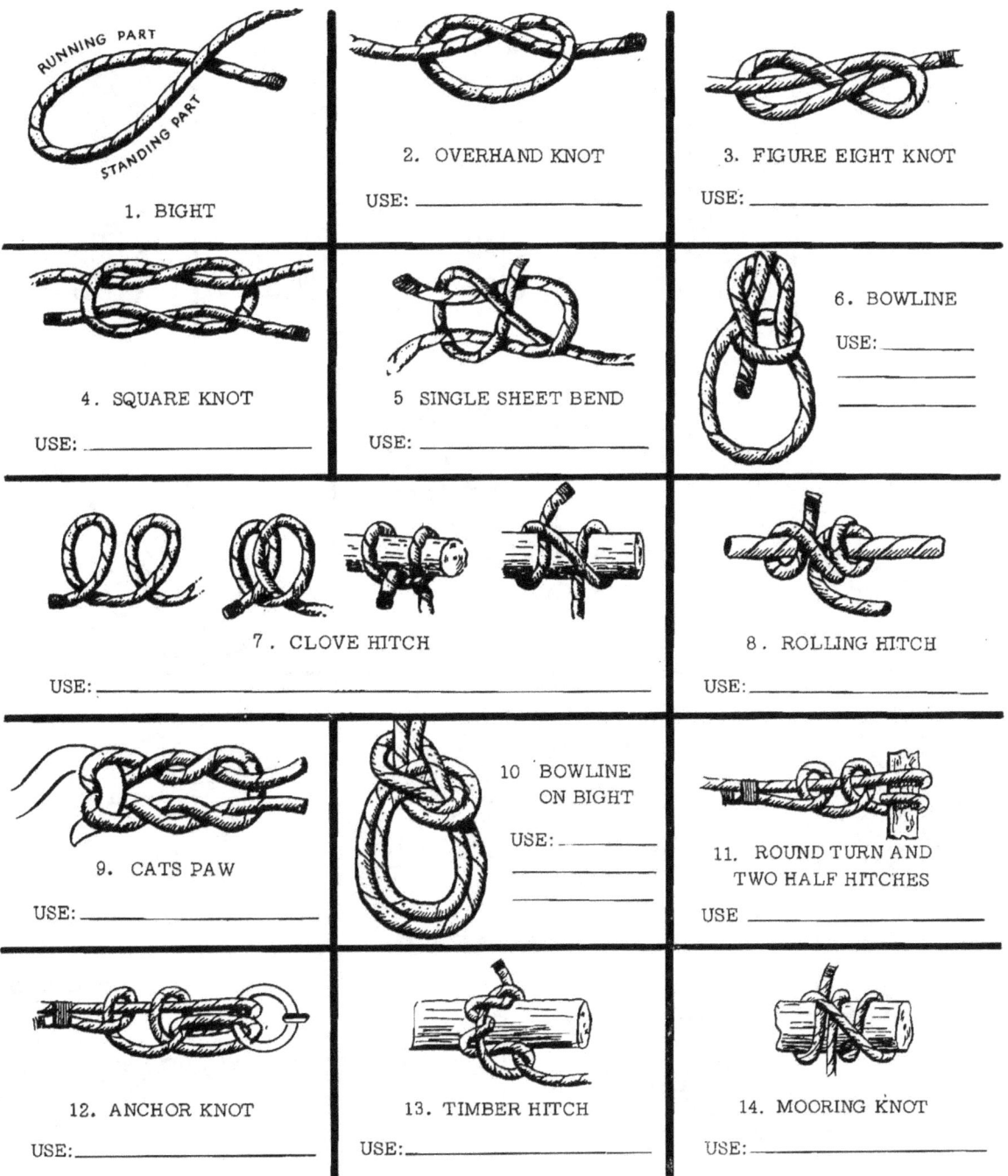

1. BIGHT
2. OVERHAND KNOT   USE: _____
3. FIGURE EIGHT KNOT   USE: _____
4. SQUARE KNOT   USE: _____
5. SINGLE SHEET BEND   USE: _____
6. BOWLINE   USE: _____
7. CLOVE HITCH   USE: _____
8. ROLLING HITCH   USE: _____
9. CATS PAW   USE: _____
10. BOWLINE ON BIGHT   USE: _____
11. ROUND TURN AND TWO HALF HITCHES   USE _____
12. ANCHOR KNOT   USE: _____
13. TIMBER HITCH   USE: _____
14. MOORING KNOT   USE: _____

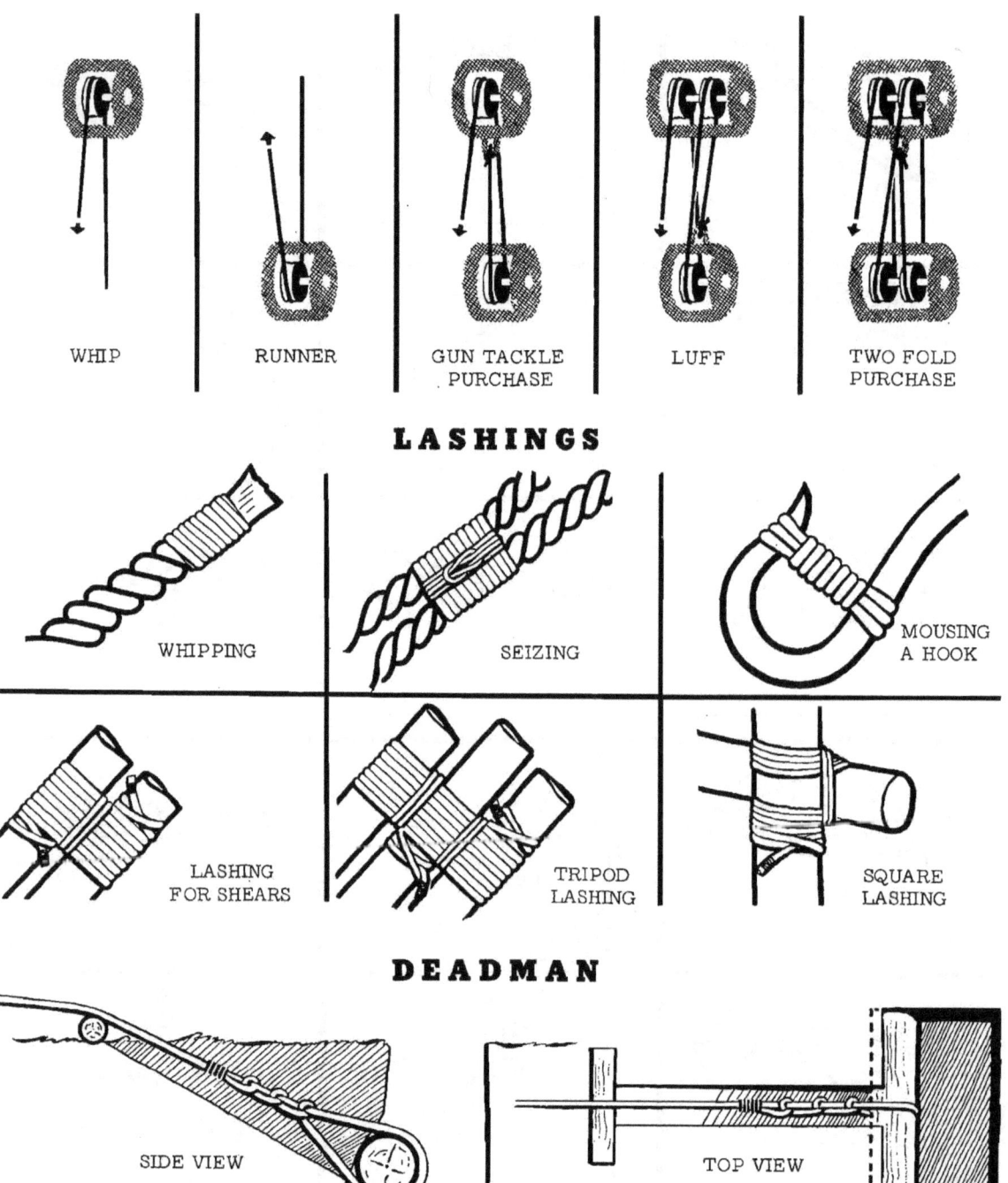

# HOISTING DEVICES

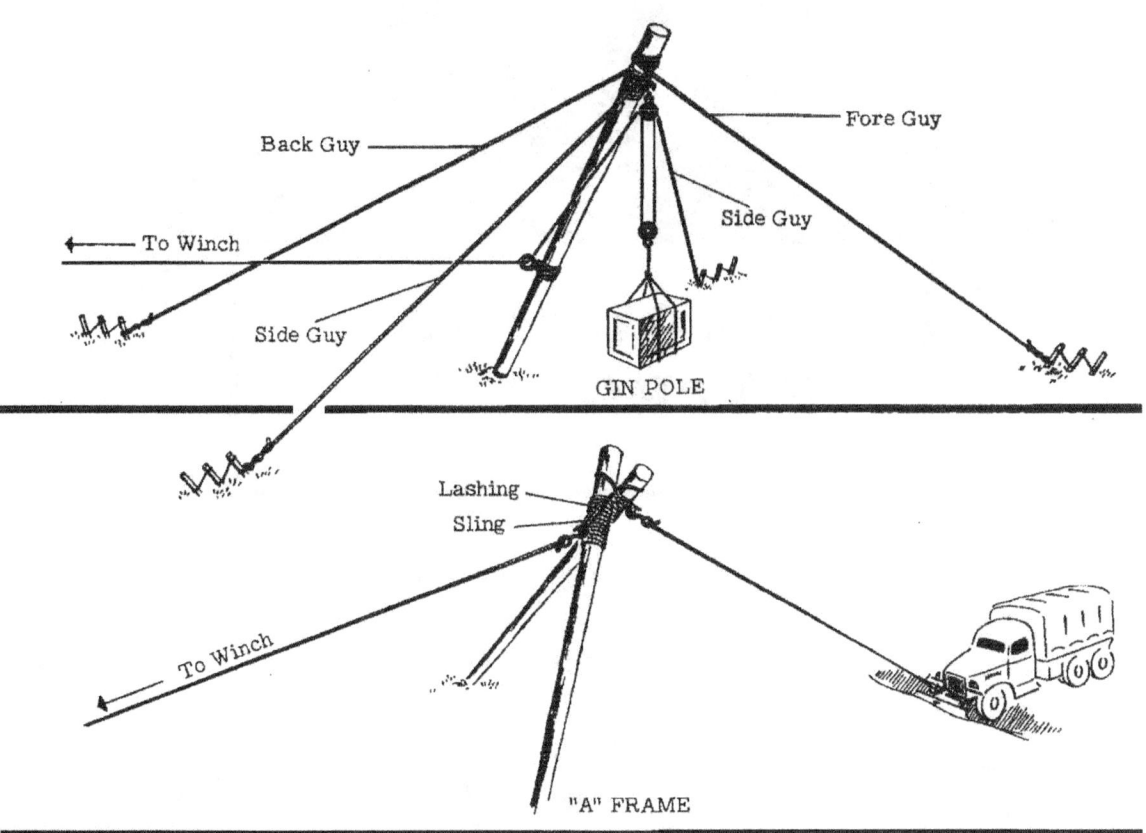

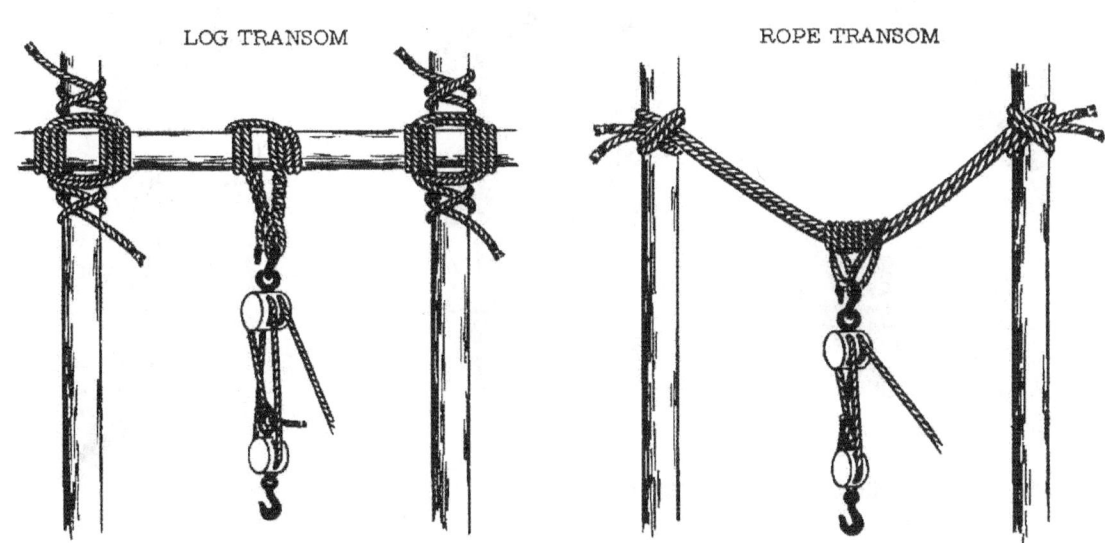

# SCOUTING, PATROLLING

Successful operation is dependent largely on information obtained by scouts and patrols.

## 3 DON'TS:

**DON'T FORGET YOUR SHADOW**
Shadows stand out when viewed from the air. Reduce your's to a minimum.

**DON'T MAKE A SILHOUETTE**
Avoid leaving the sky your background. Observe from a shaded or hidden position.

**DON'T LOOK UP**
Don't look up at aircraft or flares. Your face will show up like a headlight.

# HINTS TO SCOUTS

**EAR TO GROUND**
Sounds travel better through the ground and may be heard by pressing ear to surface.

**DOG TAGS**
The tinkle of your dog tags may disclose your position. Wrap them with tape or cloth.

**DON'T SNEEZE**
To control a sneeze, press forefinger tightly under nostrils, push back and up.

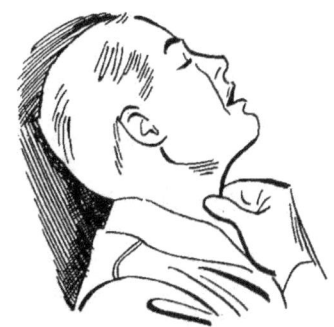

**DON'T COUGH**
Press lightly on the adam's apple. CAUTION: not too much as it will only cause more coughing.

**BLURRED VISION**
Close eyes slowly and keep them shut for a few seconds. Open them slowly and the blur is gone.

**DON'T SNIFFLE**
Make sure no one with a cold is in your patrol. A simple sniffle may cost you your life.

**OWL EYES**
Your eyes can be made more sensitive at night by forming a shield around them. The shield cuts out stray light.

**WHISPERING**
Don't whisper unless conversation is absolutely necessary. If you must whisper, then exhale a part of your breath.

**DON'T LIGHT A MATCH**
The light of a match can be seen for 10 miles. Don't let a German or Jap line up his sights on you at night.

## BY DAY:

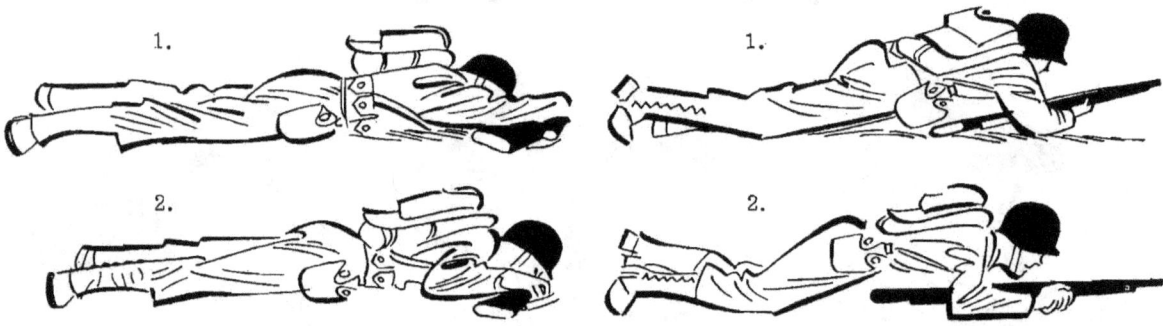

**CRAWL LIKE THIS:**
The arms are used for moving. Extend the arms and drag the body to them. Keep head and buttocks down, or you will be exposed to enemy fire.

**CREEP LIKE THIS:**
Both arms and legs are used in creeping. NO part of the body is raised off the ground. Movement is slow but much safer.

## BY NIGHT:

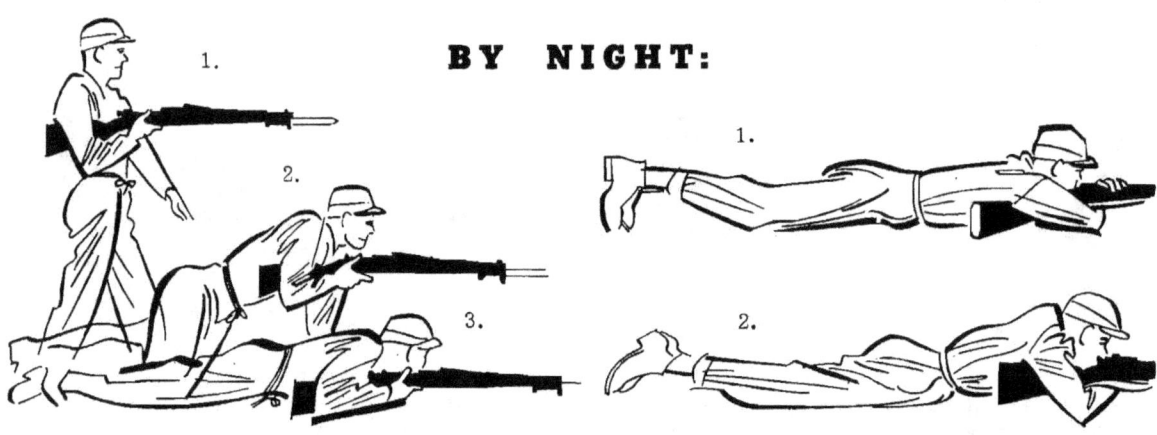

**HIT THE GROUND QUIETLY:**
Your left knee hits first, left hand is next, then the body. Don't hit with a thump. Let your weight down gradually.

**USE THE BELLY CRAWL:**
Your weight should rest on forearms! Shoulders may be slightly raised. The rifle is cradled in the arms. Fairly rapid progress may be obtained.

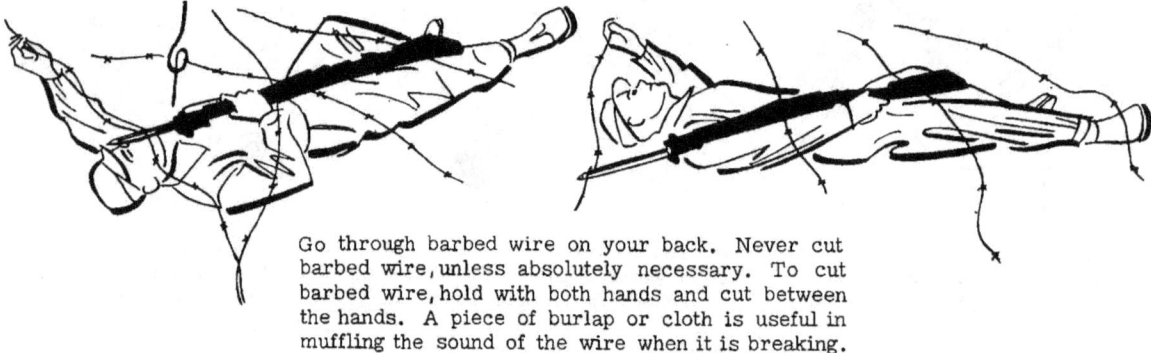

Go through barbed wire on your back. Never cut barbed wire, unless absolutely necessary. To cut barbed wire, hold with both hands and cut between the hands. A piece of burlap or cloth is useful in muffling the sound of the wire when it is breaking.

# MESSAGE COMMUNICATION

INFORMATION, TO BE OF VALUE, MUST REACH THE
COMMANDING OFFICER AT THE PROPER TIME. IT
MUST BE ACCURATE AND COMPLETE.

Communication is the nerve center of any military operation. Messages may be written, oral, or in code. They may be transmitted by voice, radio, wire, or messengers. It is essential that each communication be sent through the proper channels so that it will reach the proper place at the proper time. Information can be of two types-fact or opinion. Messages based on fact are of far greater use than those based on opinion. Oral messages are dangerous-they must be memorized.

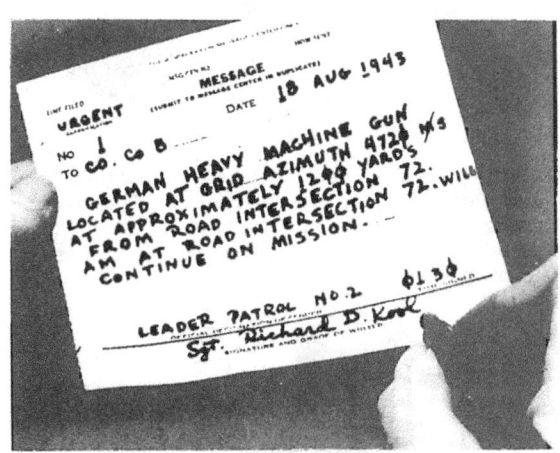

BASE MESSAGE ON FACT

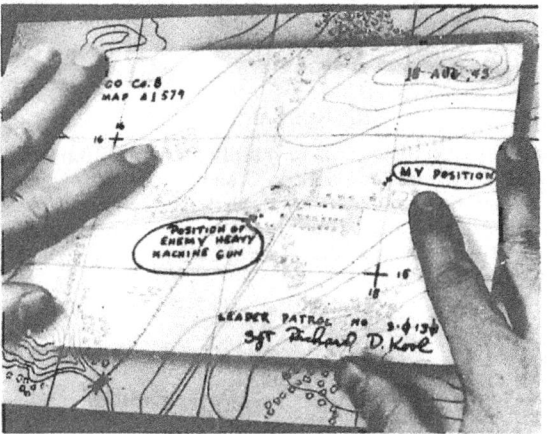

MAKE OVERLAYS BRIEF AND ACCURATE

Written messages should be prepared with great care. Accuracy and clarity of meaning cannot be over-emphasized. The message should be short but complete. Don't let an uncrossed "T" cause your message to lose its meaning.

Whenever possible use an overlay. They offer a quick, accurate and concise method of transmitting the information you desire to send. Don't waste time. Your message may save lives.

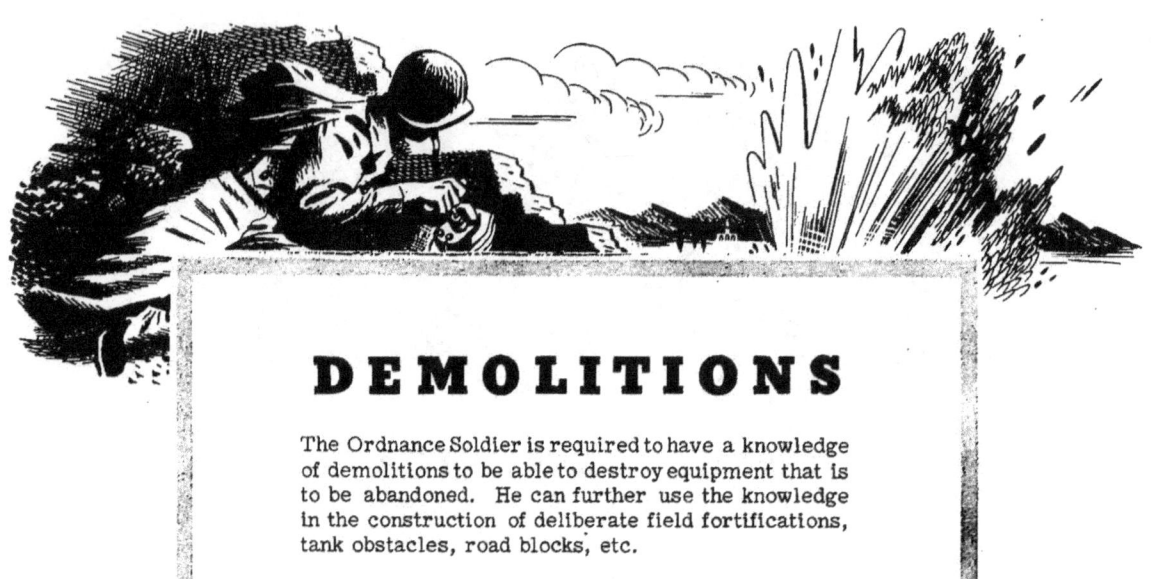

# DEMOLITIONS

The Ordnance Soldier is required to have a knowledge of demolitions to be able to destroy equipment that is to be abandoned. He can further use the knowledge in the construction of deliberate field fortifications, tank obstacles, road blocks, etc.

DYNAMITE—

TNT    NITROSTARCH    COMP. C and C2

NON-ELECTRIC    ELECTRIC

Military explosives used mainly in demolition work are: TNT and Composition C and C2 are waterproof and can be used under water: Nitrostarch and Dynamite are affected by moisture, but can be used under water by the use of waterproofing compound or grease.

Military explosives are best set off by blasting caps, either electrically or non-electrically. The electric blasting cap is detonated by either a line current or dry cell batteries. The non-electric blasting cap is detonated by using Safety Fuse.

SAFETY FUSE

PRIMACORD

Safety Fuze burns at an average rate of two feet per minute. It is used to provide a time interval so that the user may get away safely. Warning: Safety Fuze should not be confused with Primacord.

Primacord is a flexible fabric tube containing a high explosive core which explodes instantaneously. Unlike SafetyFuse, it must be detonated with a blasting cap.

# PREPARATION OF CHARGES

NON-ELECTRIC    ELECTRIC

A Primer Charge is prepared by inserting a blasting cap within the high explosive. The blasting cap is tied to prevent slipping out.

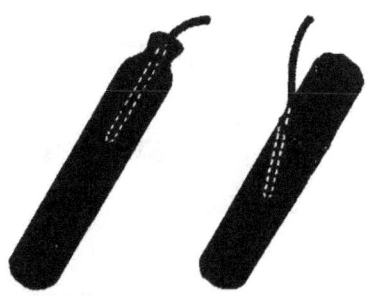

TOP    SIDE

In Dynamite the hole for the cap is made with the punch end of the Cap Crimper, found in the platoon demolition chest.

To explode several charges simultaneously, electric blasting caps may be connected in series, or Primacord can be used with one cap.

SIMULTANEOUS DETONATION

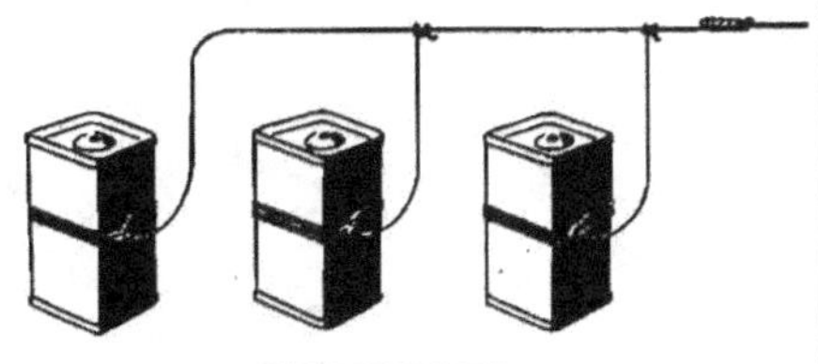

PRIMACORD

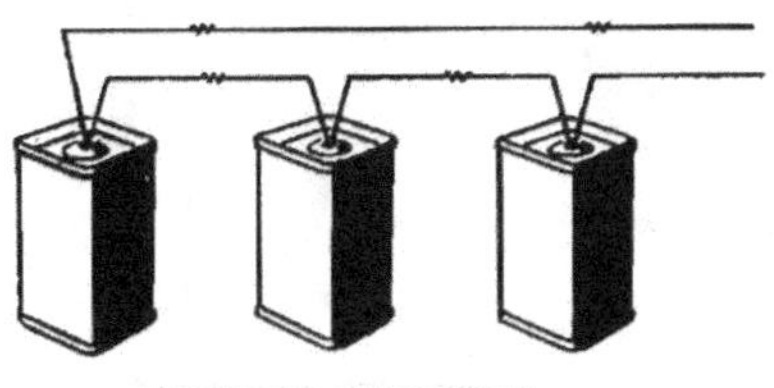

SERIES CIRCUIT

# BOOBY TRAPS

The Ordnance Soldier, in the combat zone, frequently encounters Booby Traps left by the enemy. They are to be found in abandoned equipment; in houses connected to furniture, doors, windows, etc; buried in the ground connected to inviting souvenirs; and in innumerable other places where you are least likely to expect them.

Don't be a "Booby"! Examine outdoor areas for trip wires or disturbed ground surfaces. In buildings or abandoned equipment, move nothing until it has been thoroughly examined. Trace electric circuits before using them.

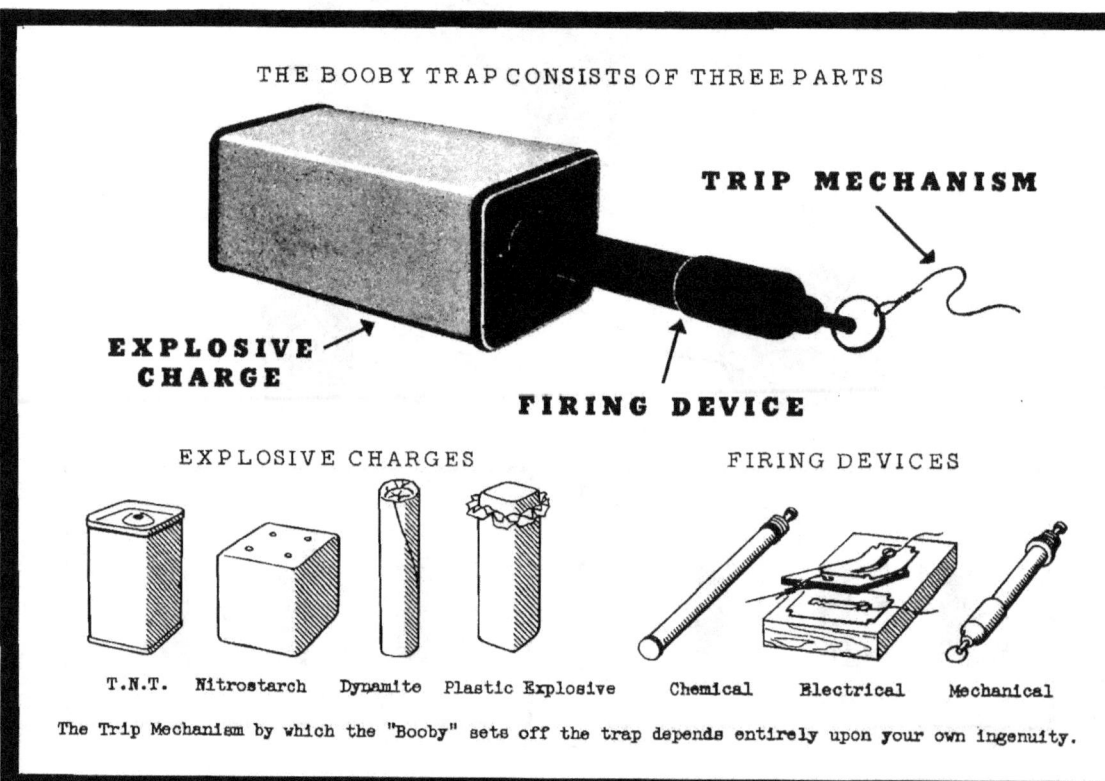

THE BOOBY TRAP CONSISTS OF THREE PARTS

EXPLOSIVE CHARGE — TRIP MECHANISM — FIRING DEVICE

EXPLOSIVE CHARGES: T.N.T., Nitrostarch, Dynamite, Plastic Explosive

FIRING DEVICES: Chemical, Electrical, Mechanical

The Trip Mechanism by which the "Booby" sets off the trap depends entirely upon your own ingenuity.

# ELECTRIC FIRING DEVICES

Electric Firing Devices are usually improvised, such as the one illustrated (Fig. 3). The simple pressure type is illustrated at right (Fig. 1).

NOTE: The nails wrapped around the explosive are for shrapnel effect and will be used in all cases.

An Electric Booby Trap (Fig. 2) can be installed in a piano so that when a particular note is struck - BOOM!

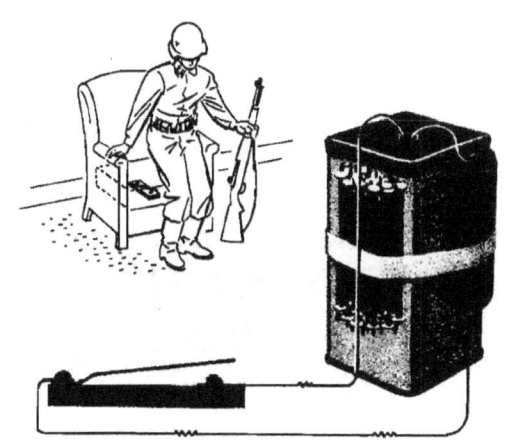

Figure 1.

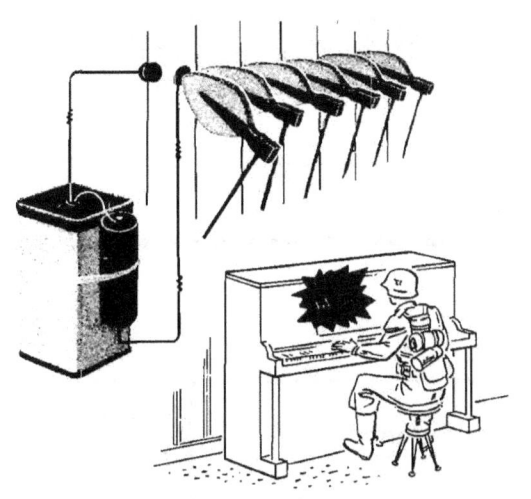

Figure 2.

Figure 3.

# CHEMICAL FIRING DEVICES

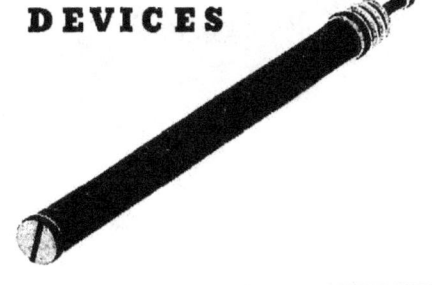

These have proven costly to manufacture and are dangerous for even the using unit to handle. Therefore those that are made are used mostly in delay mechanisms.

Acid eats thru a wire in a predetermined length of time allowing the firing pin to spring forward and set off the trap.

# MECHANICAL FIRING DEVICES

The three types of mechanical devices illustrated below have been effectively used to harass and demoralize the enemy. NOTE: A hand grenade may be used in place of a regular explosive.

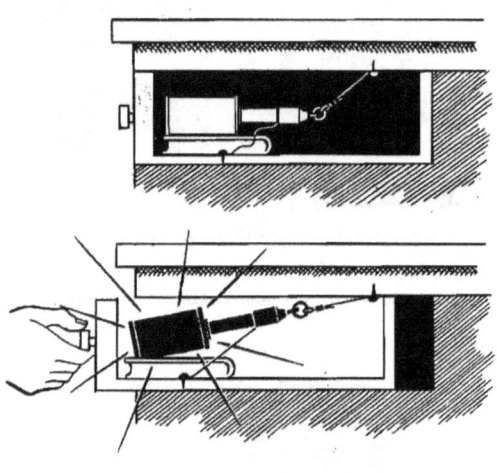

1. PULL TYPE

2. PRESSURE TYPE

3. RELEASE TYPE

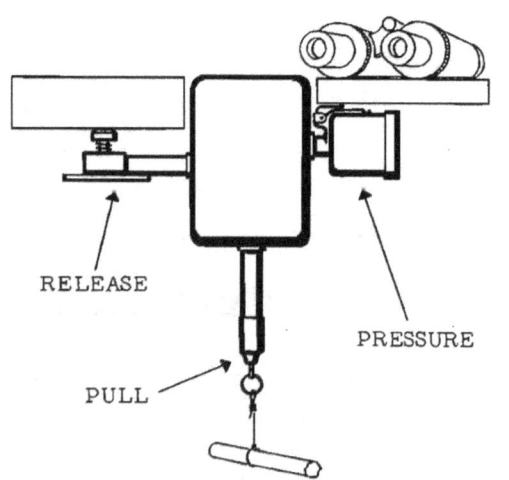

Any or all three mechanical firing devices may be used with the Antipersonnel Mine, M3.

Another effective American Antipersonnel Mine is the M2A1. When set off it jumps into the air and explodes 3 to 6 feet above ground.

A cross section view of the M2A1 Antipersonnel Mine is shown on page 88.

---

The German equivalent is the "S" Mine, which was nicknamed the "Bouncing Baby" by Americans in Africa. A point worth remembering is that the "S" Mine does not explode in midair until 4-1/2 seconds after the primer "pops". So when you hear that "pop" fall flat to the ground.

  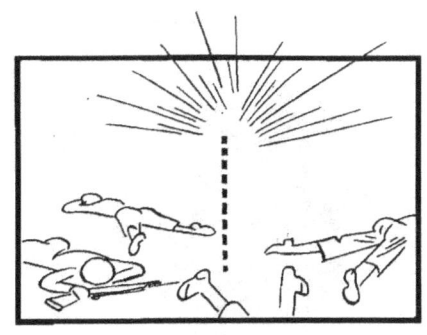

# PRECAUTIONS

DON'T BE CURIOUS!   KNOW WHAT YOU'RE DOING!

WHEN IN DOUBT - STAY OUT!   DON'T PICK UP SOUVENIRS!

SUSPECT EVERYTHING OF BEING BOOBY TRAPPED!

# KILL

## HOW TO DESTROY A JAP OR A GERMAN WITH YOUR BARE HANDS

A QUICK JERK . . .

A STRAIGHT-FINGERED BLOW . . .

A SHARP BLOW . . .

A STIFF-KNEED JUMP . . .

**. . . ALL WILL KILL**

# ATTACK THESE POINTS:

- BRIDGE OF NOSE
- POINT OF JAW
- ADAM'S APPLE
- BASE OF SKULL
- ANY POINT OF SPINE
- CROTCH
- SHIN
- INSTEP
- KIDNEYS
- SOLAR PLEXIS

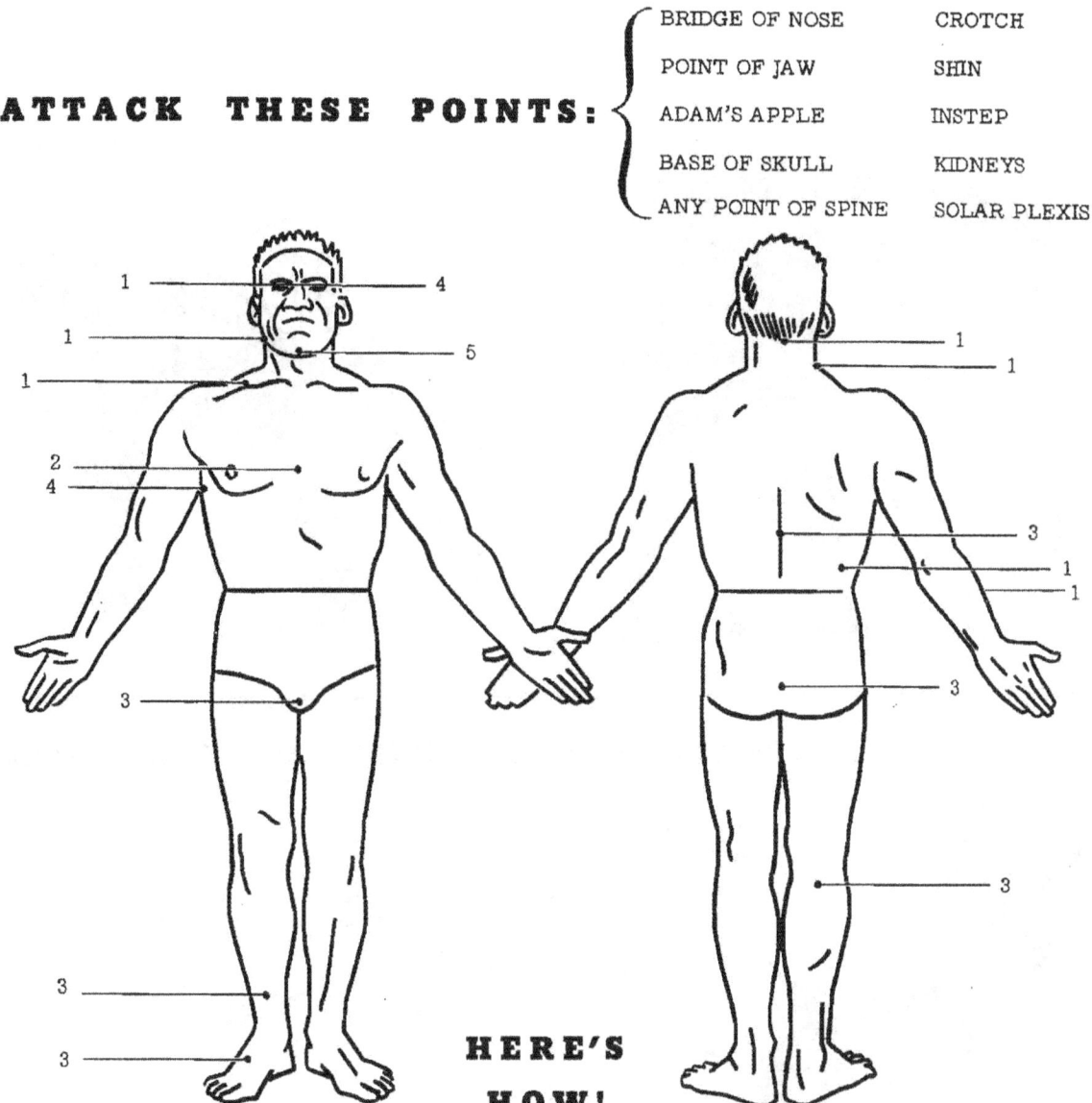

## HERE'S HOW!

1. A SHARP BLOW WITH THE OUTER EDGE OF THE HAND.
2. A SHARP BLOW WITH FIST OR ELBOW.
3. A KICK WITH THE FOOT OR THE KNEE.
4. PRESSURE WITH THE THUMBS OR FINGERS.
5. A BLOW WITH THE HEEL OF THE HAND.

## USE LEVERAGE

A QUICK JERK WILL BREAK HIS ARM

LEVERAGE AGAINST THE JOINT WILL BREAK HIS ARM

## MAXIMUM STRENGTH AGAINST MINIMUM STRENGTH

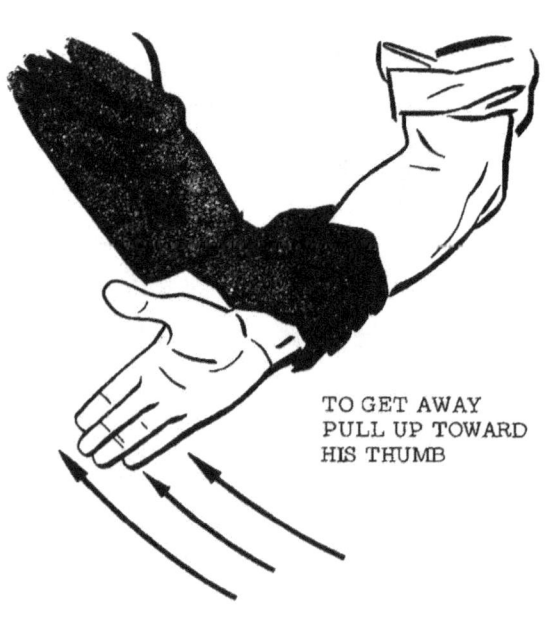

TO GET AWAY PULL UP TOWARD HIS THUMB

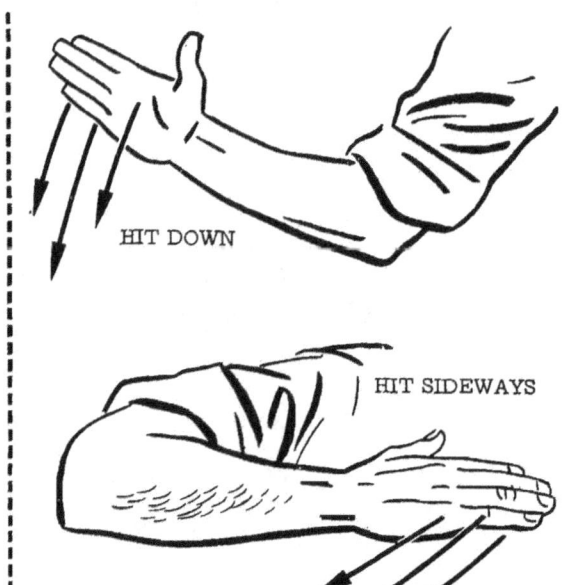

HIT DOWN

HIT SIDEWAYS

## UPSET HIS BALANCE

PULL HIM OVER BACKWARDS

THROW HIM OVER YOUR HIP

## USE HIS MOMENTUM

MAKE HIM RUSH YOU...

THEN!

# ORGANIZATION OF THE OFFICE CHIEF OF ORDNANCE

The mission of the Ordnance Department is the design, development, procurement, storage, supply, and maintenance of all Ordnance Materiel; and for the training of Ordnance military personnel.

## THE GENERAL OFFICE

The General Office coordinates the activities of its divisions and the Office, Chief of Ordnance — Detroit toward the accomplishment of the mission of the Ordnance Department.

## FIELD SERVICE DIVISION

The Field Service Division stores and issues Ordnance Materiel; inspects, repairs, alters and maintains it in the hands of troops and in storage; controls the supply of spare parts; prepares and reviews technical manuals; and reviews training manuals.

## INDUSTRIAL DIVISION

The Industrial Division procures, produces, inspects and accepts all Ordnance materiel and spare parts, and is responsible for all related engineering work, construction of new manufacturing plants and the conversion and expansion of existing plants needed for procurement.

## TECHNICAL DIVISION

The Technical Division is responsible for programs of research and development of new and improved Ordnance materiel and improved materials for Ordnance use.

## MILITARY TRAINING DIVISION

The Military Training Division is responsible for the training of Ordnance military personnel, including publication of training doctrine, scheduling of training programs, conducting and supervision of training, and assignment, selection and relief of training personnel.

## OFFICE, CHIEF OF ORDNANCE - DETROIT

The Office, Chief of Ordnance — Detroit constitutes the operating portion of the General Office concerned with the development, design, manufacture, storage, supply and maintenance of tanks, self-propelled mounts, motor, combat, and transport vehicles.

# ORDNANCE MATERIEL

| | | |
|---|---|---|
| 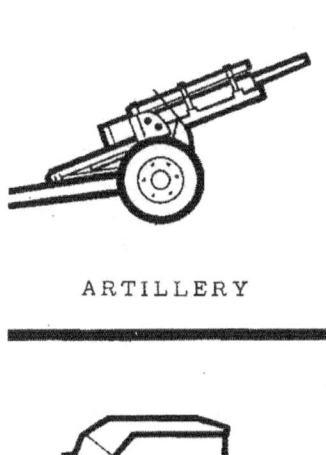 ARTILLERY | 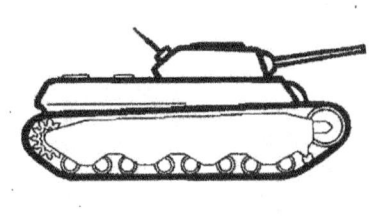 COMBAT VEHICLES |  SMALL ARMS |
|  GENERAL PURPOSE VEHICLES |  SPECIAL PURPOSE VEHICLES | 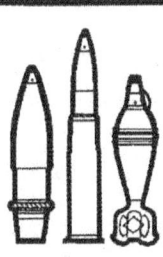 ARTILLERY AMM. |
| 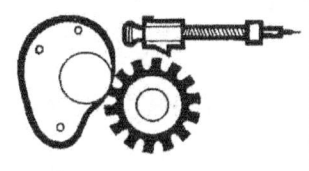 SPARE PARTS | 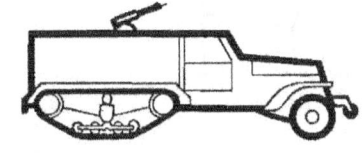 TRACK-LAYING VEHICLES |  SMALL ARMS AMM. |
| 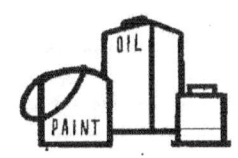 CLEANING AND PRE-SERVING MATERIALS | 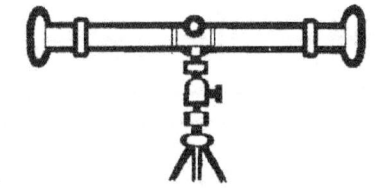 FIRE CONTROL EQUIPMENT | 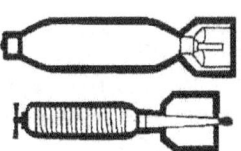 AIRCRAFT AMM. |

# ORDNANCE SERVICE IN THE FIELD

To perform field service in the combat zone, Ordnance organizations are assigned to division, corps, army, or air force units. Ordnance service is rendered by four principal types of units: Maintenance, Depot, Evacuation, and Ammunition.

### MAINTENANCE UNITS

Maintenance units supply and maintain Ordnance equipment. Supply is accomplished by drawing Ordnance materiel from depots and reissuing it to the using arms. Maintenance is speeded by exchanging serviceable items for unserviceable items; the unserviceable items are repaired or sent to the rear.

A maintenance organization may be light, medium, heavy, or base depending on the technical skill of its personnel, the tools and spare parts which it carries, and the time required to do a job.

Tire repair, vehicle assembly, vehicle distributing, railway artillery, and bomb disposal organizations render such ordnance service in the field as their names indicate.

### DEPOT UNITS

A depot unit is responsible for the supply of Ordnance general materiel to maintenance organizations. Supplies flow from base depots in the Communications Zone to Army Ordnance depots, mobile field depots, and finally to maintenance companies.

### EVACUATION UNITS

Evacuation units transport damaged materiel from the front line or collecting points to the rear for repair. They are equipped with 40-ton tank recovery units. Evacuation units are also used to transport new and repaired materiel to the front.

SUPPLY, MAINTENANCE AND EVACUATION OF GENERAL MATERIEL

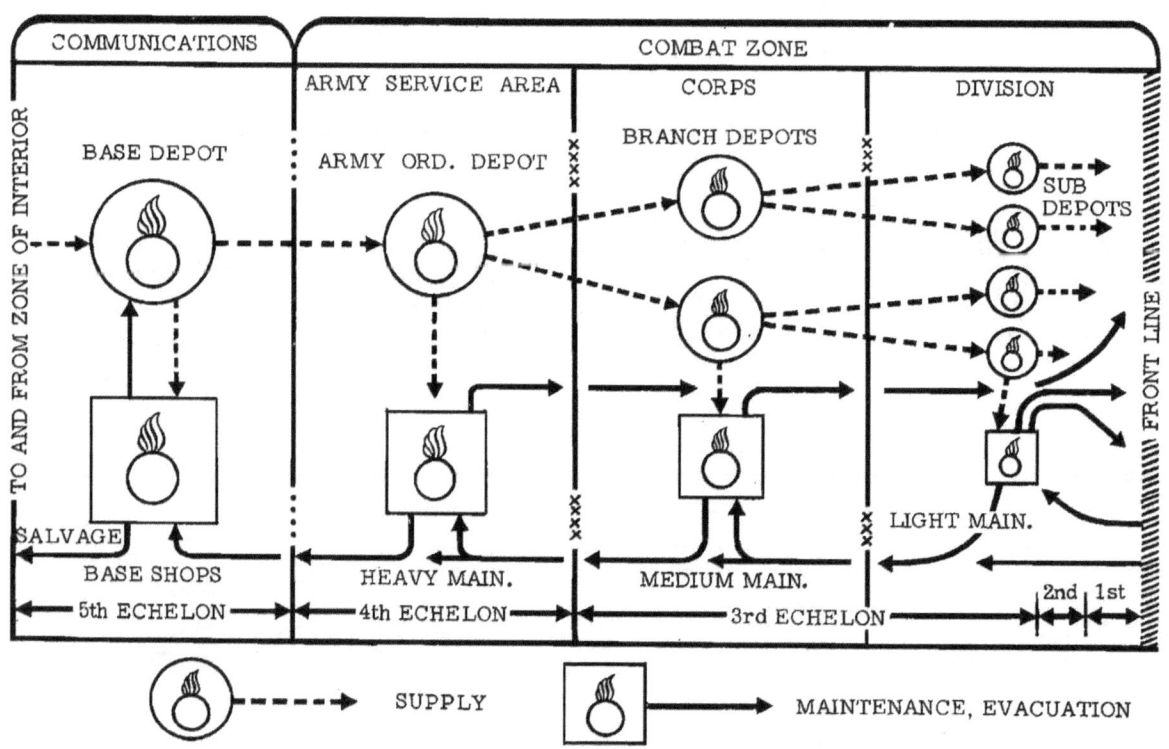

# AMMUNITION SUPPLY

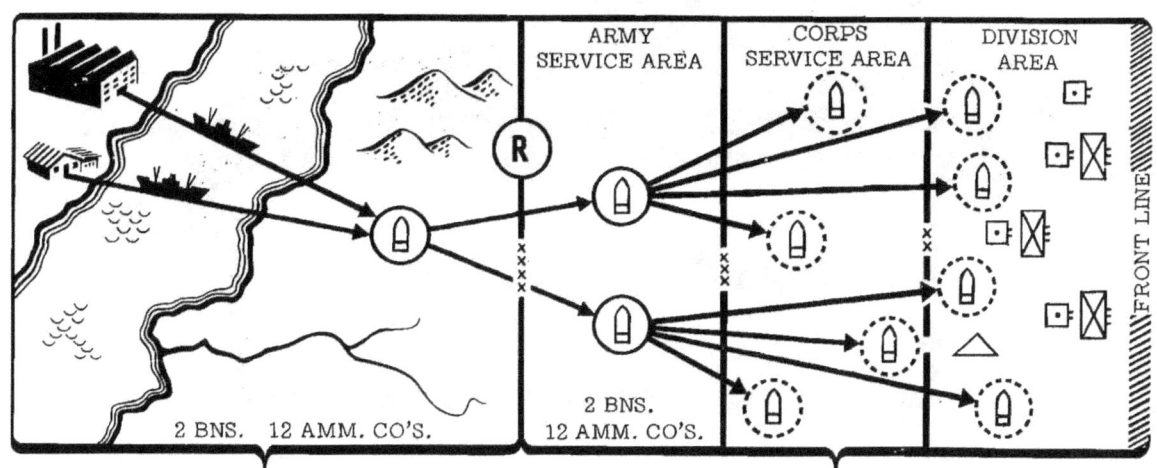

Ammunition alone constitutes the greatest mass of supplies brought to the front lines for combat troops. It is a huge job, and you are a part of the organization which must perform this job. It is the responsibility of the Ordnance Department to establish and maintain ammunition supply points in every theatre of operations and to procure and distribute ammunition to these establishments.

Let us assume that the Ordnance Department has a shipload of ammunition on the way to troops in a foreign theatre of operations. After a hazardous journey the supply ship will stop at some strategic port where the ammunition will be unloaded and classified and stored in an ammunition depot in the Communications Zone (see chart). Such a depot will be operated by Ordnance personnel. It will be huge because it will be taking the place of our large arsenals in the United States.

As ammunition is needed by our armies in the Combat Zone, it will be transported by railroad or truck to army ammunition depots located in the rear of the Combat Zone. These Army Depots must furnish ammunition to troops located in the Army Service Area and to all supply points in forward areas of the Combat Zone.

The Ordnance Department will operate the Army Depots and will establish Ammunition Supply Points (commonly called ASP's) in the Corps Service Area and the Division Area of the Combat Zone. It is these ASP's that will serve our fighting troops. It

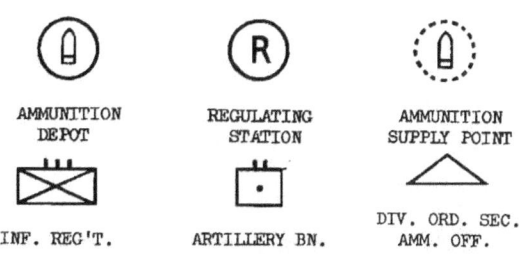

is our job to keep the ASP's stocked with types of ammunition they will need when they need it.

For each army operating in a Combat Zone there are provided two ammunition battalions, totaling twelve ammunition companies, to operate the Army Depots and ASP's. In the Communications Zone there are needed two ammunition companies for each 15-days' supply per army.

Each ammunition company has the following subdivisions which perform the duties listed:

HEADQUARTERS: Military administration, mess, supply, and transportation.
ASP OFFICE: Supervises ASP operation; prepares reports and keeps necessary records.
MAGAZINE PLATOON: Performs the physical receipt, storage, and issue of ammunition.
SERVICE PLATOON: Performs all miscellaneous duties such as guard, guide, and traffic control. Supervises shipping and receiving.

# SMALL ARMS

## HAND AND SHOULDER WEAPONS

### I. DEFINITIONS

A. **SMALL ARMS** - Normally all weapons with a bore diameter of 6/10 of an inch or less.

B. **ARMORER** - A small arms mechanic, normally applied to using arm personnel.

C. **BORE** - Inside of barrel.

D. **RIFLING** - Threading in bore to spin projectile (lands & grooves).

E. **CALIBER** - Bore diameter measured from land to land. Example: Cal. .50 equals 1/2" or .50 inches.

F. **MILIMETER** - Metric system of measurement, 25.4mm equals 1 inch.

G. **MUZZLE** - Front end of barrel.

H. **BREECH** - Rear end of barrel.

I. **CHAMBER** - That part of the breech in which the cartridge seats.

J. **MUZZLE VELOCITY** - Speed of projectile as it leaves the barrel.

### II. CYCLE OF OPERATION

A. FIRING  _____

B. UNLOCKING  _____

C. EXTRACTING  _____

D. EJECTING  _____

E. COCKING  _____

F. FEEDING  _____

G. LOADING  _____

H. LOCKING  _____

MANUALLY OPERATED WEAPONS

### III. RIFLE, U.S., CAL. .30, M1903

A. Development from the Mauser Rifle.

B. MODIFICATION.

| 1. | 2. | 3. |
|---|---|---|
| RIFLE, U.S., CAL. .30, M1903A1. | RIFLE, U.S., CAL. .30, M1903A3. | RIFLE, U.S., CAL. .30, M1903A4. |
| Differences from M1903 | Differences from M1903A1 | Difference from M1903A3 |
| 1._____ | 1._____ | 1._____ |
| 2._____ | 2._____ | USE _____ |
| 3._____ | 3._____ | _____ |
| _____ | 4._____ | 2._____ |

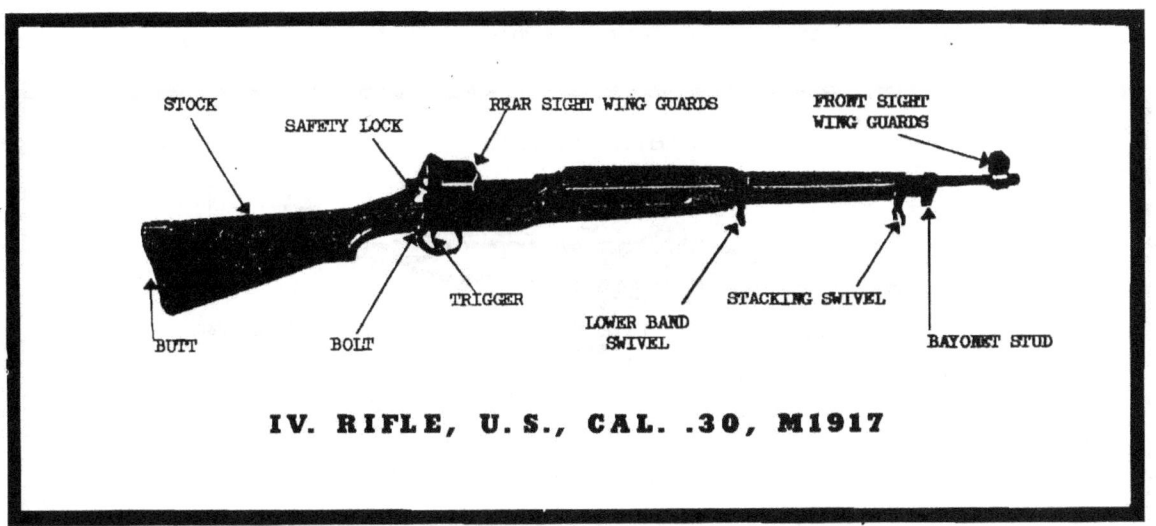

### IV. RIFLE, U.S., CAL. .30, M1917

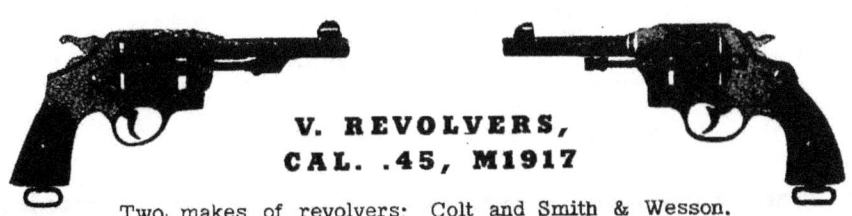

### V. REVOLVERS, CAL. .45, M1917

Two makes of revolvers: Colt and Smith & Wesson.

## VI. PYROTECHNIC PISTOLS AND GROUND PROJECTORS

A. DEFINITION OF PYROTECHNICS.
1. Modifications of fireworks to produce a brilliant light for illumination, or colored lights or smoke for signalling.

B. USE OF PYROTECHNIC PISTOLS.
1. To send signals from _____ or _____ .

C. USE OF PYROTECHNIC GROUND PROJECTORS.
1. To send signals from _____ .

## VII. GAS OPERATED WEAPONS

A gas operated weapon is one which uses the gas generated by the burning of the propellant charge to operate the weapon.

A. A gas operated weapon is either semi-automatic or full-automatic.

1. In semi-automatic weapons the cycle of operation is completed automatically except for _____ .
2. In full-automatic weapons all the steps in a complete cycle of operation are performed automatically.

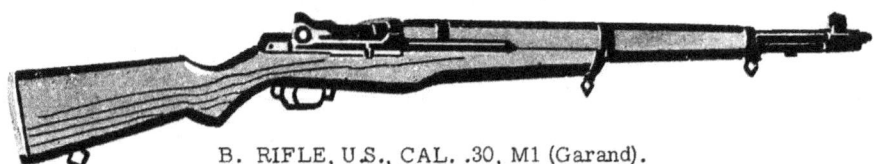

B. RIFLE, U.S., CAL. .30, M1 (Garand).

1. Gas operated, semi-automatic, aircooled, shoulder weapon.

2. The receiver holds a clip of _____ rounds.

3. In case of a misfire the weapon may be cocked by rotating the _____ .

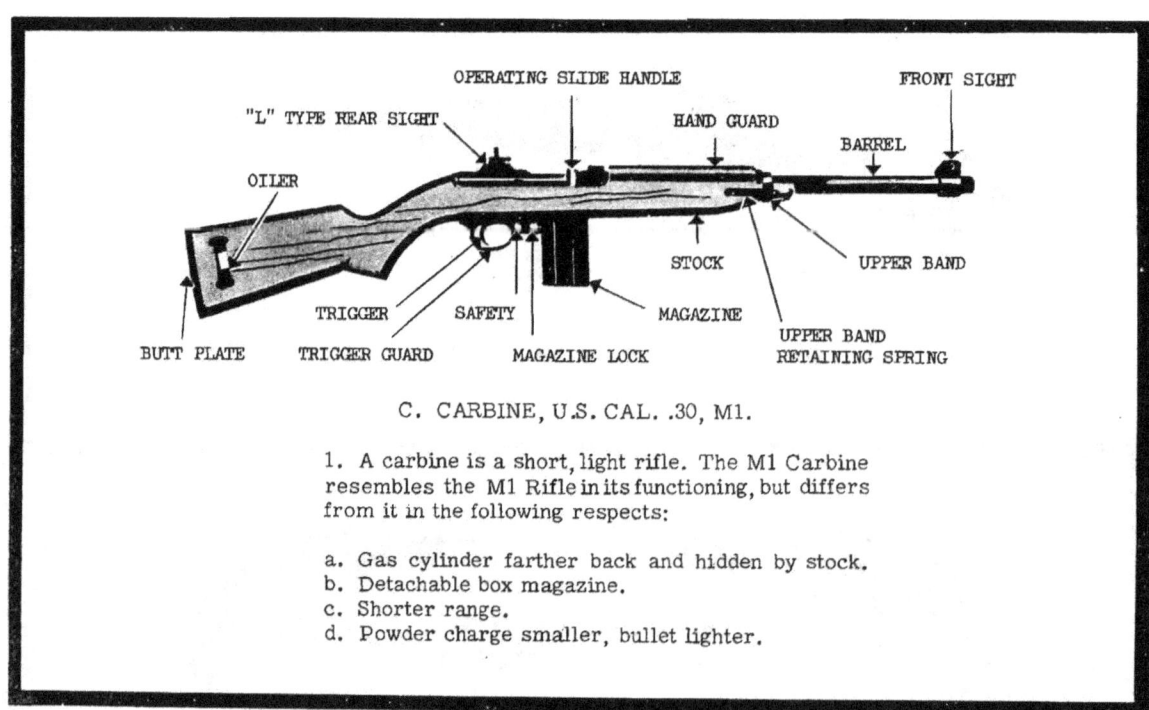

C. CARBINE, U.S. CAL. .30, M1.

1. A carbine is a short, light rifle. The M1 Carbine resembles the M1 Rifle in its functioning, but differs from it in the following respects:

a. Gas cylinder farther back and hidden by stock.
b. Detachable box magazine.
c. Shorter range.
d. Powder charge smaller, bullet lighter.

## VIII. RECOIL OPERATED WEAPONS
(Semi-automatic)

Recoil operated weapons derive the energy to operate the weapon from the force of the powder gas on the base of the cartridge causing the bolt and barrel to move. In a recoil operated weapon the barrel moves to permit the _____ to leave the barrel before the _____ is unlocked from the barrel.

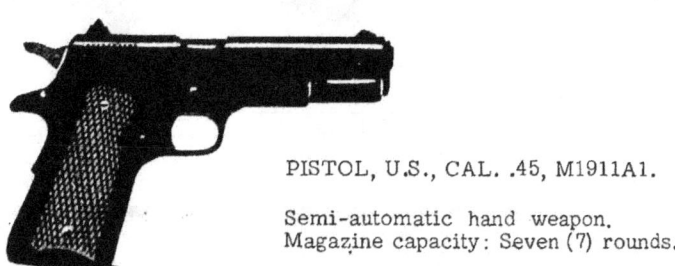

PISTOL, U.S., CAL. .45, M1911A1.

Semi-automatic hand weapon.
Magazine capacity: Seven (7) rounds.

---

## IX. BLOWBACK OPERATED WEAPONS

THOMPSON SUB-MACHINE GUN, M1928A1.
A. Blowback operation is similiar to _____ except barrel _____
B. May be fired semi-automatic or full-automatic.

C. Reasons why weapon fires from an open bolt:

1. _____

2. _____

---

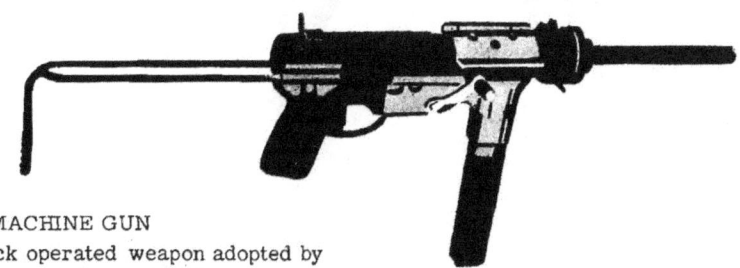

M-3 SUB-MACHINE GUN
A. Blowback operated weapon adopted by U.S. Army — easy to manufacture.
B. Fires Full-automatic only.

# SMALL ARMS (cont'd)

1. BROWNING AUTOMATIC RIFLE:

   A. The B.A.R. is a _____ weapon which fires from an _____.
   B. The model 1918A2 fires either _____ or _____.
   C. The B.A.R. is fed from a _____.

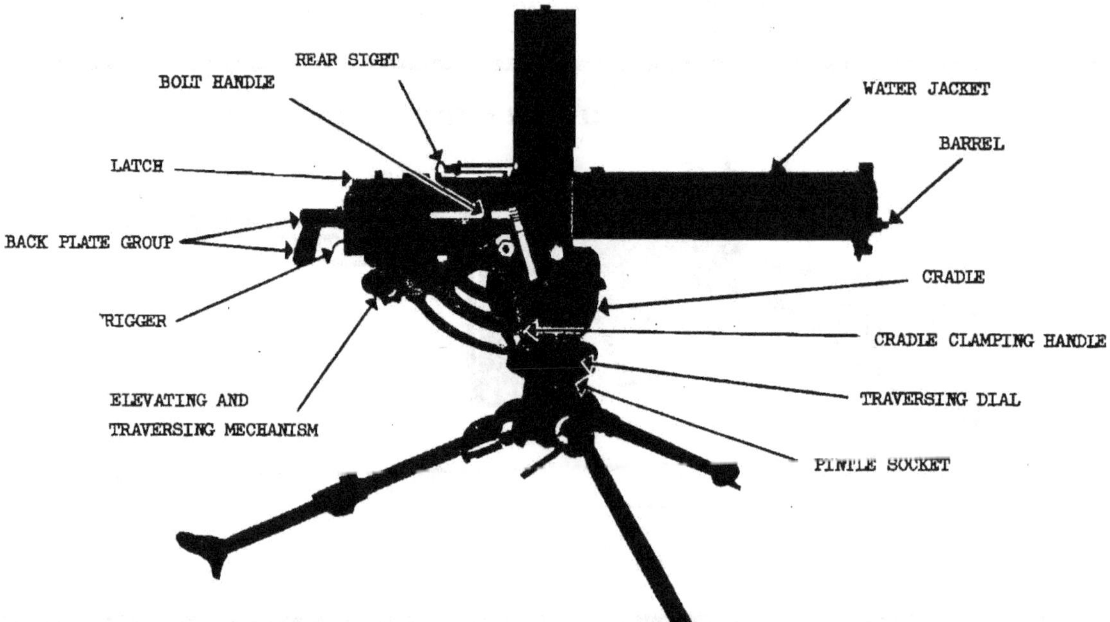

2. BROWNING MACHINE GUN CAL. .30 M1917:

DEVELOPMENT:
1. Developed by Browning and adopted by U. S. Army in 1917.
2. Standard model is now M1917A1.
   a. Moderate changes were made in receiver.

DESCRIPTION:
B.M.G. M1917A1 is a _____, _____, _____, _____ weapon:

USE:
Chiefly used as a defensive weapon against infantry.

## III. BROWNING MACHINE GUN, CAL. .50, M2

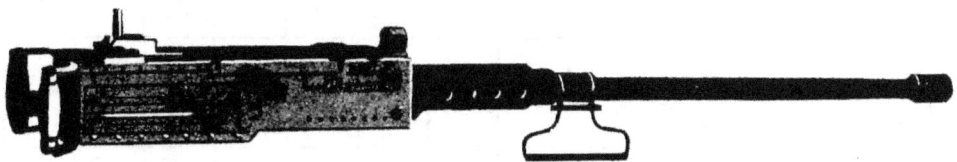

### B. HEAVY BARREL
Use: Used by ground forces against armored vehicles and also in armored vehicles.

### A. WATERCOOLED
Use: Chiefly used as an antiaircraft weapon.

---

## IV. BROWNING MACHINE GUN, CAL. .30, M1919A4

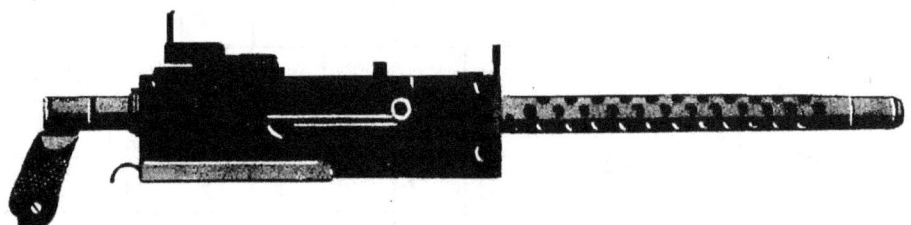

| A. | B. | C. |
|---|---|---|
| DIFFERS FROM M1917A1 IN FOLLOWING RESPECTS: | USE: | MODIFICATIONS: |
| 1._____ | 1. Offensive, defensive, ground weapon. | 1. M1919A5 used in M3 tank. |
| 2._____ | 2. In armored vehicles. | 2. M1919A6 same as 1919A4 but uses a bipod mount and shoulder stock. Has lighter, tapered barrel. |
| 3._____ | | |

---

### DIFFERENCES BETWEEN LONG AND SHORT RECOIL OPERATED WEAPONS:

In long recoil operated weapons, barrel and bolt are locked together. The recoil distance of the barrel is approximately equal to the length of the cartridge. The breech mechanism is unlocked by the bolt being held back while the barrel returns to its forward position.

In short recoil operation, bolt or slide and barrel are locked together. The recoil distance is very short (in U.S. Pistol M1911, barrel distance is approximately 3/8"). The barrel stops and unlocks from the slide while the slide continues to the rear.

| | Pistol, Auto. Cal. .45, M1911A1 | Carbine, M1 Cal. .30 | U.S. Rifle, Cal. .30 M1 | B.A.R. Cal. .30 M1918A2 | Submachine Gun Cal. .45, M1928A1 | U.S. Rifle Cal. .30 M1903A1 | B.M.G., Cal. .30 M1917A1 | B.M.G., Cal. .30 M1919A4 | B.M.G., Cal. .50 M2, W.C. | B.M.G., Cal. .50 M2, H.B. |
|---|---|---|---|---|---|---|---|---|---|---|
| **TOTAL** Weight (Lbs) | 2.43 | 5.2 | 9.5 | 22 | 10.8 | 8.75 | 41 | 30.5 | 100 | 84 |
| **TOTAL** Length (In) | 8.5 | 36 | 43.6 | 47.8 | 33.7 | 43.46 | 38.64 | 41.25 | 66 | 65 |
| **BARREL** Weight | 0.2 | | 3.65 | | 0.75 | 24 | 3 | 7.35 | 15.2 | 29.5 |
| **BARREL** Length | 5.03 | 18 | 24.07 | 24 | 10.54 | 24 | 23.9 | 24 | 45 | 45 |
| **RIFLING** Lands | | 4 | 4 | 4 | 6 | 4 | 4 | 4 | 8 | 8 |
| **RIFLING** Grooves | 6 | 4 | 4 | 4 | 6 | 4 | 4 | 4 | 8 | 8 |
| **RIFLING** One turn per | 16" | 20" | 10" | 10" | 16" | 10" | 10" | 10" | 15" | 15" |
| **RIFLING** Type | L.H. | R.H. | R.H. | R.H. | R.H. | R.H. | R.H. | R.H. | R.H. | R.H. |
| **AMMUNITION** Type | B | B | B, AP, T | B, AP, T | B | B, T | B | B, AP, T | B, AP, T | B, AP, T |
| **AMMUNITION** Cal. | .45 | .30 | .30 | .30 | .45 | .30 | .30 | .30 | .50 | .50 |
| Chamber Pressure sq.in. (1000 Lbs) | 16 | 38 | 50 | 50 | 17 | 48 | 48 | 48 | 48 | 48 |
| Muzzle Velocity (Ft./Sec.) | 825 | 2000 | 2805 | 2805 | 990 | 2805 | 2805 | 2805 | 2935 | 2935 |
| Maximum Range (Yds) | 1600 | 2000 | 3450 | 3450 | 1700 | 3450 | 3450 | 3450 | 7500 | 7500 |
| Effective Range (Yds) | 75 | 300 | 600 | 600 | 75 | 600 | 1000 | 1000 | 1000 | 1000 |
| **WEIGHT (In Grains)** Powder Charge | | 110 | 152 | 152 | | 152 | 152 | 152 | 711 | 711 |
| **WEIGHT (In Grains)** Bullet | | | | | | | | | | |
| S.N.L. | B6 | B28 | B21 | A4 | A32 | B3 | A5 | A6 | A37 | A39 |
| No. Component Parts | | 15 | 50 | 50 | 5 | 50 | 50 | 50 | 250 | 250 |
| Trigger Pull (Lbs) | 5 to 6.5 | 4.6 | 5.5 to 7.5 | 6.10 | 10 to 14 | 4.5 to 6.5 | 7.7 | 7.7 | 10 to 20 | 10 to 20 |
| Life of Barrel (1000) Rds | 10 | 51 | 78 | 105 | | 91 | 146 | 160 | 263 | 196 |
| Cyclic Rate of Fire | | | | 350 to 550 | | 725 | 400 to 550 | 400 to 450 | 550 to 700 | 450 |
| Sustained Rate of Fire | | | 20 | 100 | | 100 | 250 | 150 | 400 | 75 |

Note: Column for Submachine Gun M1928A1 shows trigger pull range "10 to 14" with cyclic rate 725; rifling twist 1 turn per 16", 6 grooves/lands, R.H. Effective range values for the M1917A1, M1919A4, M2 W.C., and M2 H.B. machine guns are 250, 150, 400, and 75 respectively in sustained rate column. Some individual cell readings are uncertain due to the rotated diagonal header layout of the original page.

# AMMUNITION

## EXPLOSIVE REACTIONS

**LOW EXPLOSIVE (SLOW)**

IGNITED BY FLAME     BURNING OVER ENTIRE SURFACE     BURNING INWARD FROM ALL SURFACES

**HIGH EXPLOSIVE (FAST)**

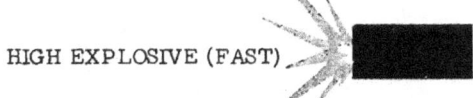     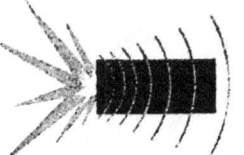    

INITIAL EXPLOSION     SHOCK WAVE     INSTANTANEOUS DETONATION THROUGHOUT EXPLOSIVE

## IMPORTANT MILITARY EXPLOSIVES

| EXPLOSIVE | TYPE | USES |
| --- | --- | --- |
| BLACK POWDER | SENSITIVE LOW | IGNITER, TIME FUSE |
| SMOKELESS POWDER | NON-SENSITIVE LOW | PROPELLANT |
| LEAD AZIDE | VERY SENSITIVE HIGH | PRIMER COMPOSITION |
| MERCURY FULMINATE | VERY SENSITIVE HIGH | PRIMER COMPOSITION |
| TNT | NON-SENSITIVE HIGH | SHELL, BOMB FILLER |
| AMATOL | NON-SENSITIVE HIGH | LARGE SHELL, BOMB FILLER |
| EXPLOSIVE "D" | VERY NON-SENSITIVE HIGH | ARMOR-PIERCING SHELL FILLER |
| TETRYL | SLIGHTLY SENSITIVE HIGH | BOOSTER |

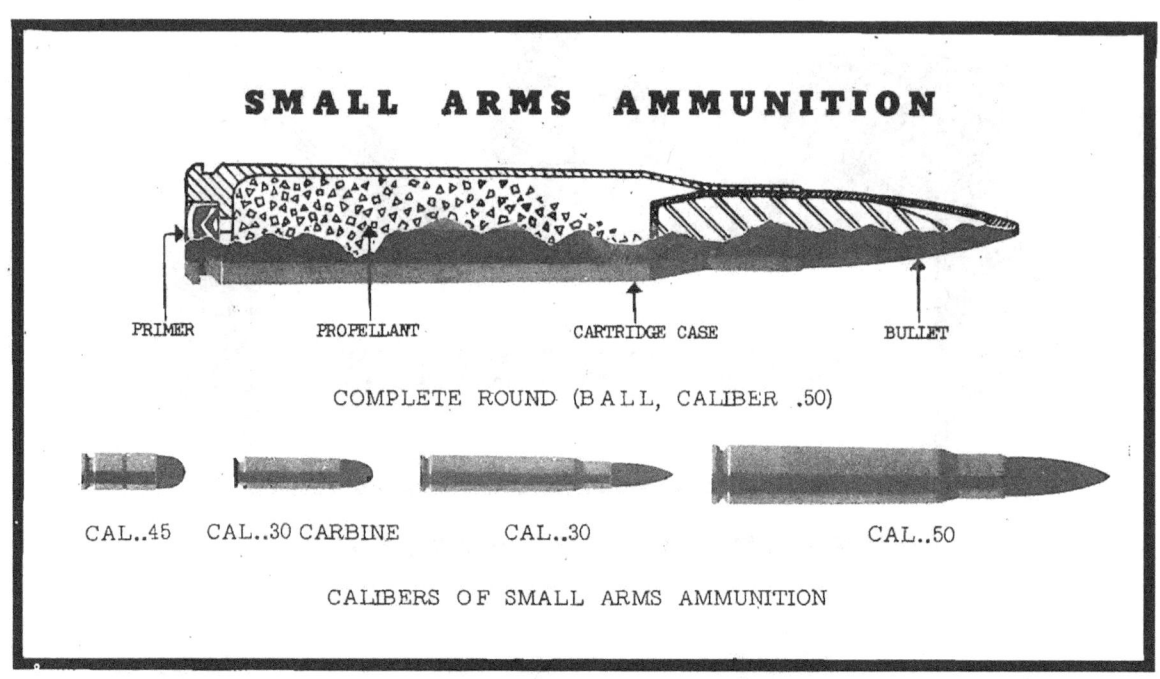
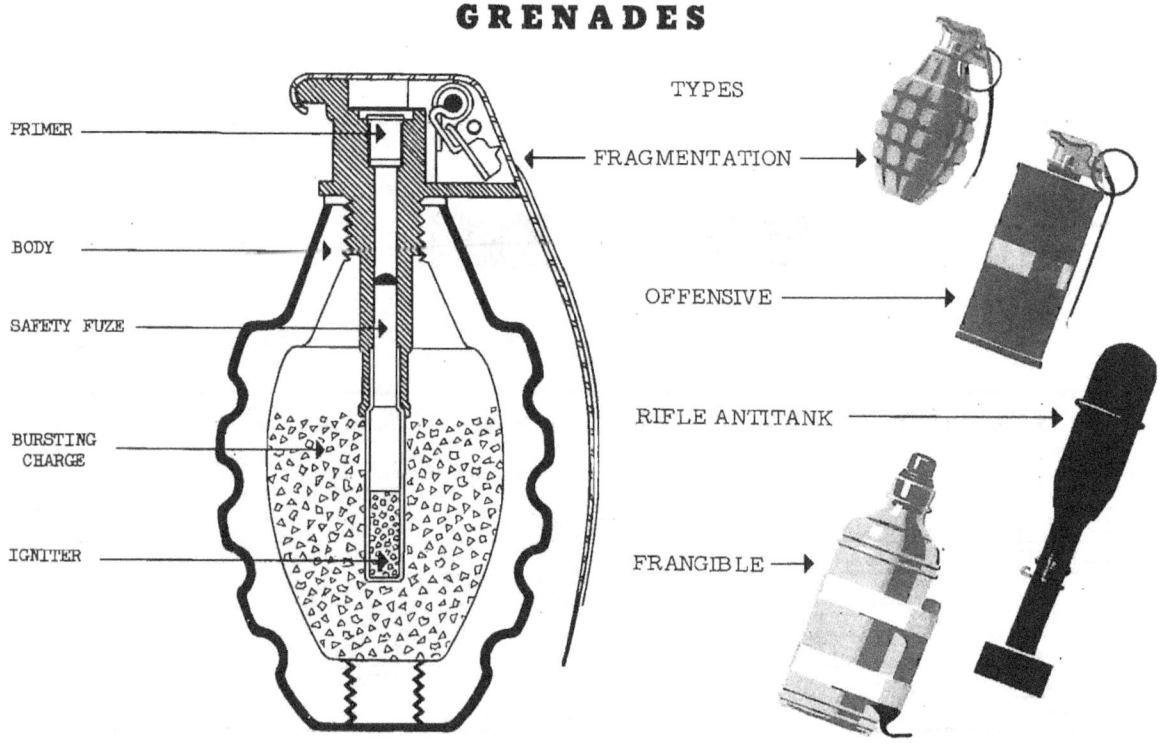

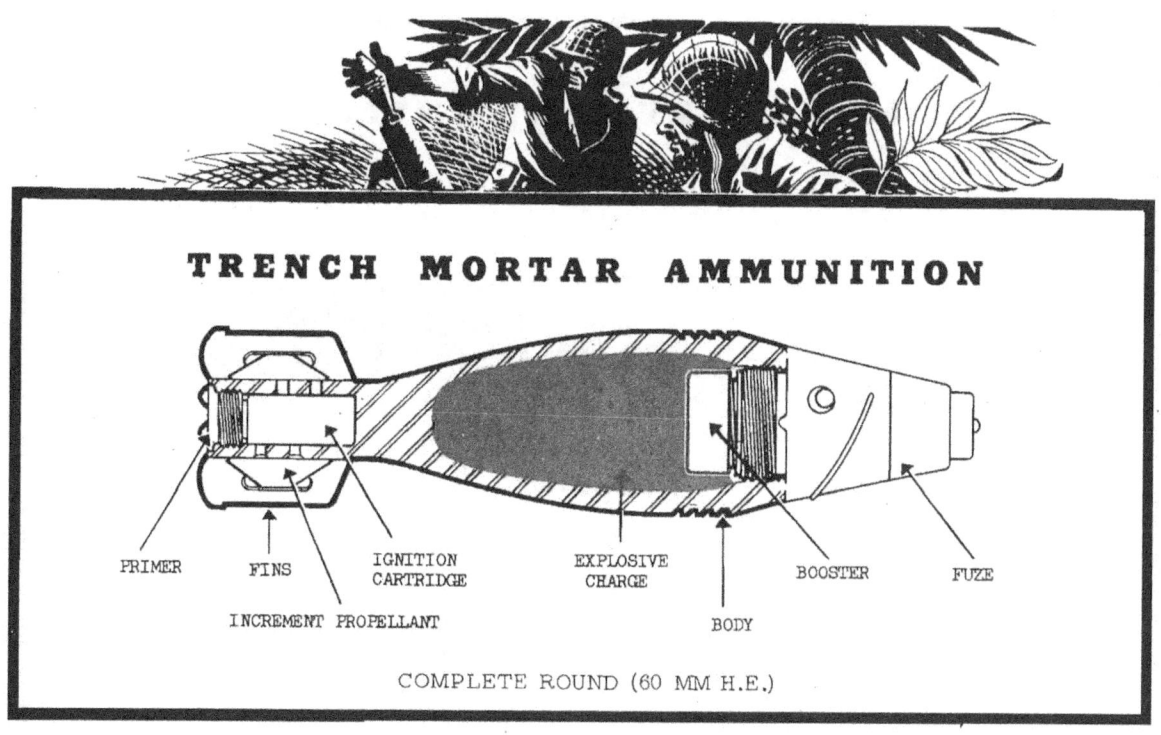

# TRENCH MORTAR AMMUNITION

PRIMER    FINS    IGNITION CARTRIDGE    EXPLOSIVE CHARGE    BOOSTER    FUZE
INCREMENT PROPELLANT    BODY

COMPLETE ROUND (60 MM H.E.)

TYPES OF TRENCH MORTAR SHELLS

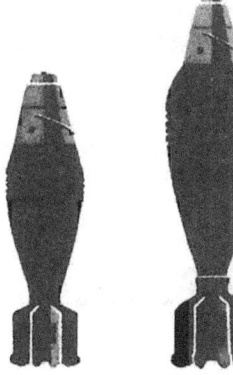

60 MM     81 MM

Light shells, high explosive and teardrop shaped, used against personnel and light targets.

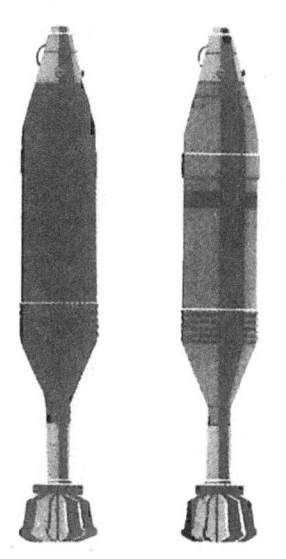

81 MM H.E.     81 MM CHEM.

Heavy shell, high explosive for demolition effect, and gas shell for smoke, etc.

60 MM ILLUMINATING

Light pyrotechnic shell for illumination of target, using parachute type flare.

# ARTILLERY AMMUNITION

COMPLETE ROUND (HIGH EXPLOSIVE SHELL)

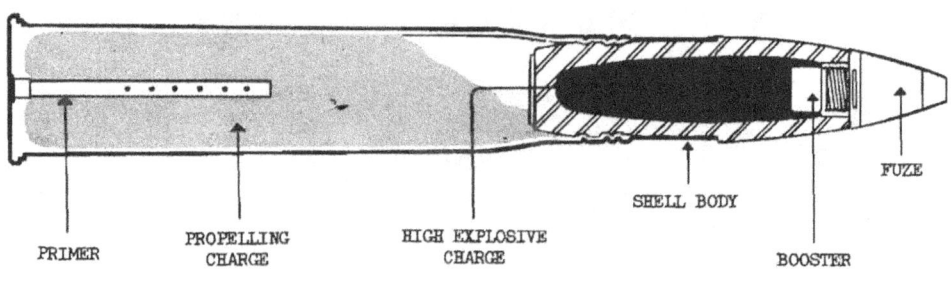

PRIMER    PROPELLING CHARGE    HIGH EXPLOSIVE CHARGE    SHELL BODY    BOOSTER    FUZE

FUNCTIONING: Primer composition ignites black powder in primer tube. Black powder flashes through holes in primer tube. Propellant is ignited, forcing projectile down bore of gun. At target, fuze functions, detonating booster, which in turn detonates high explosive charge.

THREE TYPES OF ARTILLERY AMMUNITION

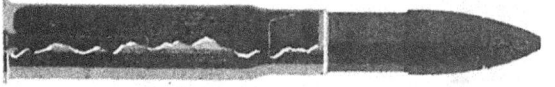

FIXED

Loaded in one operation; projectile crimped to cartridge case; propelling charge cannot be varied by gunner.

SEMI-FIXED

Projectile fits loosely into cartridge case; propelling charge contained in increment bags, can be varied by gunner.

SEPARATE LOADING

Larger caliber ammunition, loaded in three operations, 1. Projectile is inserted in breech and seated in barrel. 2. Bags of propelling charge inserted behind projectile. 3. Primer inserted in breechblock.

# ARTILLERY PROJECTILES

HE SHELL - Fuze and booster in nose detonate high explosive filler which fills shell case.

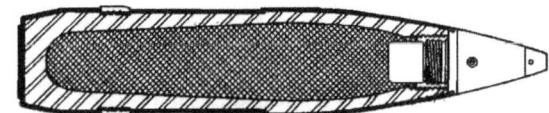

•

AP SHOT - Solid steel shot for use against armored vehicles. Contains no filler.

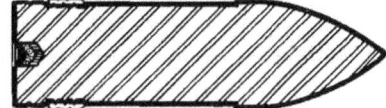

•

AP SHELL - Base fuze and booster detonate small amount of high explosive filler. Windshield on nose provides streamlining; nose cap improves armor-piercing ability.

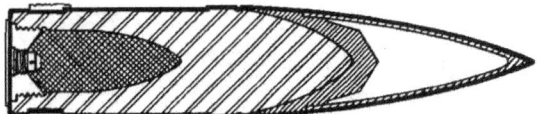

•

CHEMICAL SHELL - Nose fuze and booster detonates burster which runs through the length of the shell. Burster breaks shell body and spreads chemical filler.

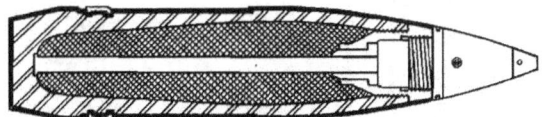

•

SMOKE SHELL - Nose fuze explodes bursting charge in nose of shell, which ignites the three smoke candles and forces them out the base of the shell.

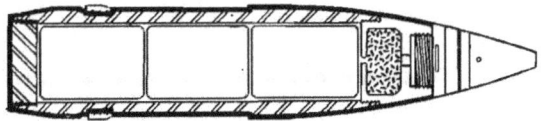

•

CANISTER - Shock of firing breaks up thin case and steel balls spread out from the muzzle of the gun with a shot gun effect.

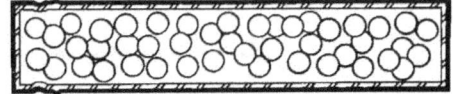

## FUZES

THE THREE TYPES OF FUZES

INSTANTANEOUS

TIME

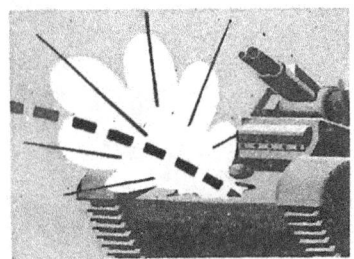
DELAY

# ANTITANK ROCKET

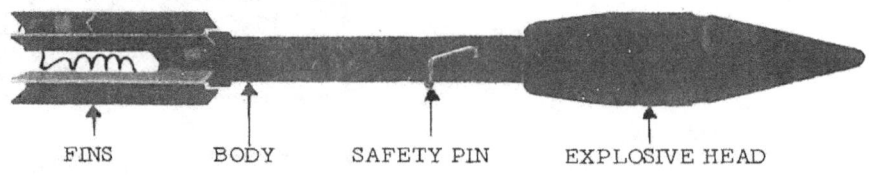

FINS  BODY  SAFETY PIN  EXPLOSIVE HEAD

# MINES

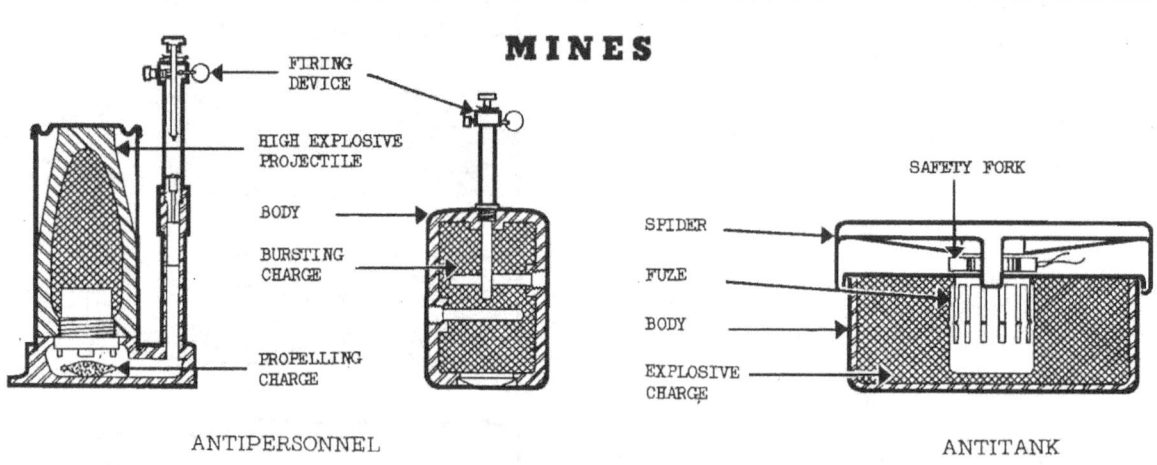

ANTIPERSONNEL  ANTITANK

# BOMBS

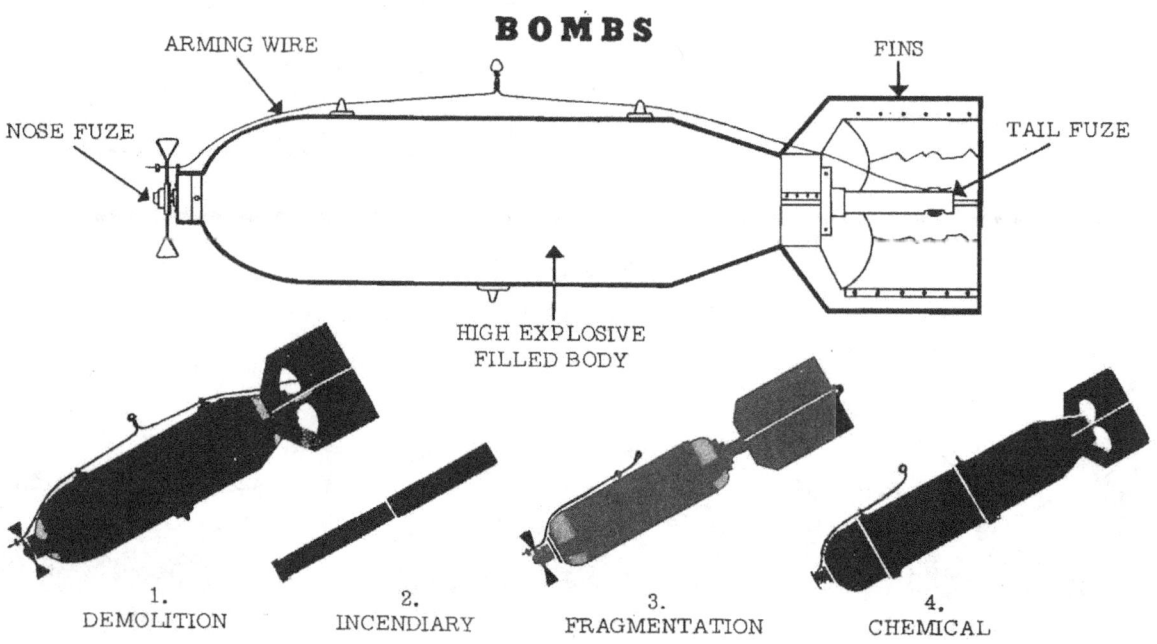

1. DEMOLITION
2. INCENDIARY
3. FRAGMENTATION
4. CHEMICAL

# ARTILLERY

THERE ARE THREE TYPES OF ARTILLERY WEAPONS:

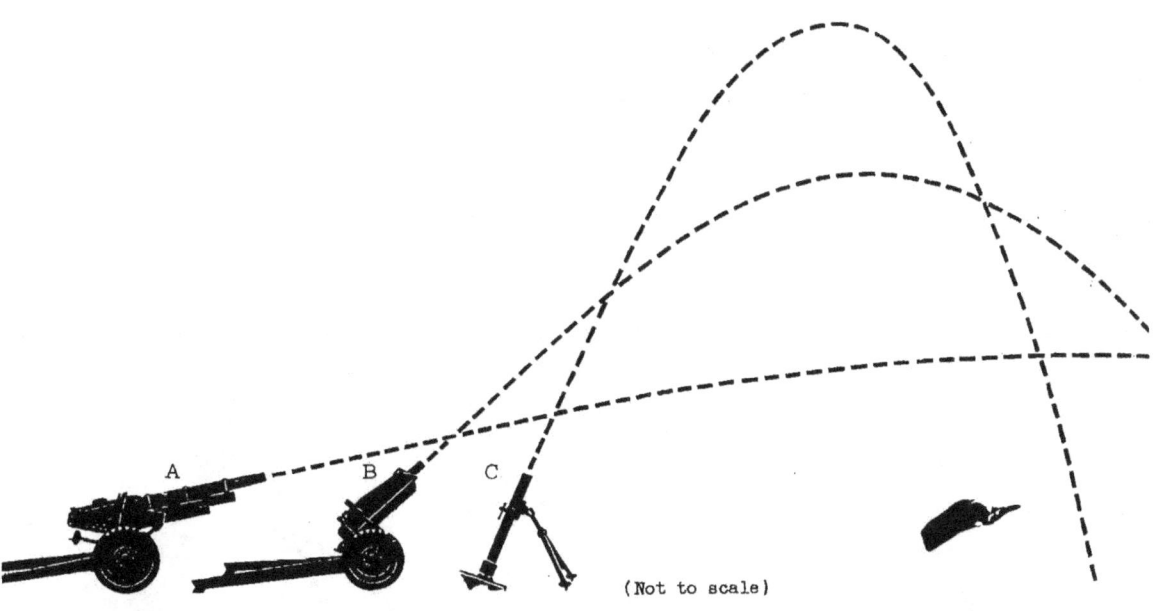

(Not to scale)

### A. GUN

1. Low, flat trajectory
2. Long tube
3. High muzzle velocity

Tank, antitank, and antiaircraft artillery weapons are always guns. They are sometimes referred to as rifles.

### B. HOWITZER

1. High angle trajectory
2. Short tube
3. Intermediate muzzle velocity

Some of our modern day howitzers serve as dual purpose weapons as both howitzers and guns.

### C. MORTAR

1. Short high trajectory
2. Stubby tube
3. Low muzzle velocity

Most mortars are smooth bore and are muzzle loaded; some large mortars are rifled and breech loaded.

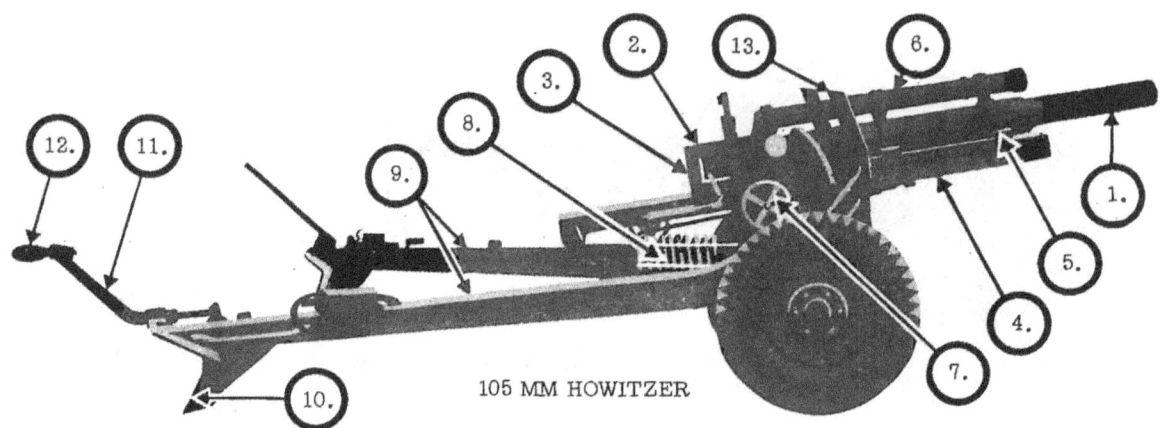

105 MM HOWITZER

COMPONENT PARTS ON AN ARTILLERY WEAPON

1. The TUBE corresponds to the barrel of a rifle.
2. The BREECH RING houses the breechblock.
3. The BREECH BLOCK is a device for closing off the breech end of the tube after ammunition has been inserted, and houses the firing mechanism.
4. The CRADLE supports the sleigh. In some weapons which do not have a sleigh it supports the tube and houses the recoil mechanism.
5. The SLEIGH is the immediate support of the tube and houses the recoil mechanism.
6. The RECOIL MECHANISM absorbs the shock of firing and returns the tube to battery. The cylinder above the tube is the counter-recoil cylinder. The recoil cylinder is below the tube - inside cradle.
7. Indicates the position of the TRUNNION which is the axis about which the tube rotates in a vertical plane, i.e., up and down.
8. The EQUILIBRATOR counteracts the unbalanced effect of placing trunnion so far to rear of tube.
9. The TRAILS hold the weapon steady during firing; provide a means for towing behind truck.
10. The SPADE digs into the ground during firing and prevents the gun from moving to the rear.
11. The DRAWBAR provides a connection between the trails and the Prime Mover, or towing vehicle.
12. The LUNETTE fits over the pintle or connecting pin on the Prime Mover.
13. The SHIELD is made of light armor plate to protect the cannoneers.

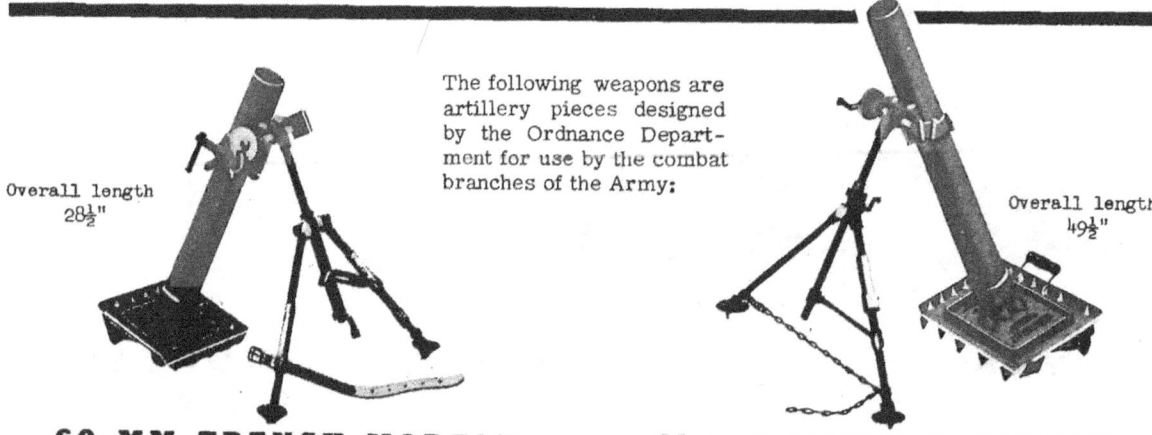

The following weapons are artillery pieces designed by the Ordnance Department for use by the combat branches of the Army:

Overall length 28½"

Overall length 49½"

### 60 MM TRENCH MORTAR

RANGE: 100 to 1985 yards  WEIGHT: 42 lbs.
TACTICAL USE: Employed by the Infantry against concealed objectives such as trenches, machine gun nests, and small installations "behind a hill".

### 81 MM TRENCH MORTAR

RANGE: 300 to 3290 yards  WEIGHT: 136 lbs.
TACTICAL USE: Same as 60 MM Trench Mortar, except it is effective for longer range and against larger installations.

### 37 MM ANTITANK GUN

RANGE: 7500 yards
WEIGHT: 912 lbs.
TACTICAL USE: Used by the Infantry against tanks, personnel.
Overall length . . . . . . 154-1/2"

### 57 MM ANTITANK GUN

RANGE: 10,000 yards
WEIGHT: 2700 lbs.
TACTICAL USE: Used by the Infantry against tanks.
Overall length . . . . . . 200-1/2"

### 75 MM PACK HOWITZER

RANGE: 9500 yards
WEIGHT: 1269 lbs.
TACTICAL USE: Used by the Field Artillery. It is broken down into six units and carried by mules or airborn troops. It is effective against concealed installations in mountainous or jungle terrain.
Overall length . . . . . . . . . 145"

### 75 MM FIELD HOWITZER

RANGE: 9500 yards
WEIGHT: 2224 lbs.
TACTICAL USE: Employed by the Field Artillery with the Cavalry Division against concealed objectives.
Overall length . . . . . . . . . 155"

### 75 MM GUN

RANGE: 13,600 yards
WEIGHT: 3460 lbs.
TACTICAL USE: Employed by the Field Artillery for direct fire against tanks and light installations.
Overall length . . . . . . . . . 220"

### 105 MM HOWITZER

RANGE: 12,150 yards
WEIGHT: 4235 lbs.
TACTICAL USE: Used by the Field Artillery as a dual purpose weapon, both gun and howitzer. This is the primary supporting weapon of the Infantry Division.

Overall length . . . . . . . . . 238"

### 155 MM HOWITZER

RANGE: 16,500 yards
WEIGHT: 12,000 lbs.
TACTICAL USE: Employed by the Field Artillery for high trajectory and counter-battery fire. 4.5 in. Gun may be mounted on this carriage.

Overall length . . . 318"

### 155 MM GUN

RANGE: 24,500 yards
WEIGHT: 29,000 lbs.
TACTICAL USE: Employed by the Field Artillery for long range fire against heavy installations. The 8 in. Howitzer may be mounted on this carriage.

Overall length . . . . . . . . . 412"

The main differences between antiaircraft and field artillery pieces are: (a.) The extreme degrees of traverse and elevation. (b.) High muzzle velocity. (c.) The remote control system of aiming.

The average range of elevation is from -5° to +90° and all antiaircraft pieces have a 360° continuous traverse. The muzzle velocity of all A.A. weapons is greater than 2600 ft. per. sec. There are two classes of antiaircraft weapons - medium which is automatic, and heavy which is manually operated. The weight of projectiles vary from 1.34 lbs. to 50 lbs. Effective ranges are from "tree top" level up to 50,000 feet.

## 40 MM AA GUN

The Bofors 40 MM Gun, and intermediate antiaircraft weapon is fully automatic. Aimed manually or by remote control; a multi-purpose weapon used against air and ground targets. Fires high explosive and armor piercing ammunition.

```
Rate of fire . . . . . . . . . . . 120 rounds per min.
Effective Range (Vertical). . . . . . . . . . 2 miles
Traverse . . . . . . . . . . . . 360 Deg. (Continuous)
Muzzle velocity . . . . . . . . . 2870 ft. per. sec.
Limits of Elevation . . . . . . . . . . -6 to + 90 Deg.
Weight of Weapon . . . . . . . . . . . . . . 5549 lbs.
Overall length . . . . . . . . . . . . . . . . . 241"
```

## 37 MM AA GUN

Is a recoil operated, automatic weapon, and sighted manually or by remote control. It is a target gun, i.e., its effectiveness depends on direct hits; fires high explosive and armor piercing ammunition.

```
Rate of fire . . . . . . . . . 120 rounds per. min.
Effective range (Vertical). . . . . . . . . . 2 miles
Traverse . . . . . . . . . . . . 360 Deg. (Continuous)
Muzzle Velocity . . . . . . . . . . 2600 ft. per. sec.
Limits of elevation . . . . . . . . . . -5 to + 90 Deg.
Weight of Weapon . . . . . . . . . . . . . . 6100 lbs.
Overall length . . . . . . . . . . . . . . . . . 225½"
```

## 90 MM AA GUN

Is used against High level bombers, and ground targets. As an A.A. gun, it fires in a battery of four, controlled by one director. As a field gun, it is manually operated using scope sights. It is not a target gun; depends on pattern of shell burst for effectiveness.

```
Rate of fire . . . . . . . 20 to 30 rounds per. min.
Effective Range (Vertical) . . . . . . . . . . 6 miles
Traverse . . . . . . . . . . . 360 Deg. (Continuous)
Length (traveling position) . . . . . . . . . . 250"
```

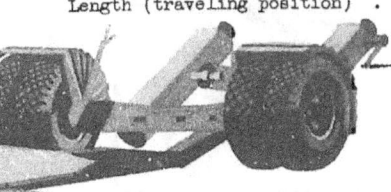

# AUTOMOTIVE

One of the biggest jobs for Ordnance soldiers is to keep the Army rolling. The Ordnance Department, of which you are a member, is charged with designing and arranging for the production of all military vehicles. They include jeeps, trucks, half-tracks, tanks, wreckers, etc. used by the different branches of the U.S. Army.

Many of you will be trained to work on these vehicles, since Ordnance provides maintenance for all of them. For example, replacing a defective starter with a new one is third echelon work which ordinarily is performed by soldier-mechanics of a maintenance company. Rebuilding this defective starter is fourth echelon work, and therefore done by a base shop or the original manufacturer (fifth echelon).

Familiarize yourself with all automotive equipment. You may be an artillery mechanic or an instrument repairman, but you may have to work on some tank or truck in an emergency. Knowing how may save your life.

## GENERAL PURPOSE VEHICLES

MOTORCYCLE

MADE BY:_____ H.P._____
USES: 1._____
2._____
3._____
TANK CONTAINS:_____ MI. PER GAL:_____
WEIGHT:_____ CYLINDERS:_____

TRUCK, 1/4 TON, 4 X 4

MADE BY:_____ H.P._____
USES: 1._____
2._____
3._____
TANK CONTAINS:_____ MI. PER GAL:_____
WEIGHT:_____ CYLINDERS:_____

# GENERAL PURPOSE VEHICLES (cont'd)

TRUCK, 3/4 TON (DODGE), 4 X 4

One of best light trucks in this war.

REPLACES:_____

USES: 1._____

2._____

3._____

TANK CONTAINS:_____  MI. PER GAL:_____

WEIGHT:_____ H.P._____ CYLINDERS:_____

TRUCK, 2-1/2 TON, 6 X 6, G M C

Purpose of original trucks: To be "prime movers" towing vehicles for artillery pieces.
Not a rear wheel suspension.

USES: 1. Cargo and/or personnel carrier.
2. Light wrecker when equipped with boom and hoist.
3. Prime mover for artillery.
4. Maintenance company shop truck and spare parts truck.

Amphibian model ("Duck") is designed for ship-to-inland service.

TANK CONTAINS: _____ MI. PER GAL:_____

WEIGHT:_____ H.P._____ CYLINDERS:_____

## COMBAT VEHICLES

SCOUT CAR, M3A1

USES: 1. Light combat.  2. Reconnaissance.
3. Personnel carrier.  4. Prime mover.

TANK CONTAINS:_____ MI. PER GAL._____

WEIGHT:_____ H.P._____ CYLINDERS:_____

ARMAMENT:_____

HALF TRACK

Transition from wheel to track vehicles. Is more adaptable for rough terrain than the Scout Car from which it was developed. The Half Track has a disengageable front wheel drive while the Scout Car's front wheels are always engaged.

TANK CONTAINS:_____ MI. PER GAL.:_____

WEIGHT:_____ H.P._____ CYLINDERS:_____

ARMAMENT:_____

# LIGHT TANKS

### LIGHT TANK T9E1

Light tanks usually have thin armor - are built for reconnaissance in force, not for hard combat.

WEIGHT:_____ ARMAMENT:_____
MI. PER GAL:_____ FRONT ARMOR:_____

### LIGHT TANK M3A3

Hull design streamlined. Armor slanted, low silhouette. Hatches and periscopes replace windshields of older vehicles.

### LIGHT TANK M5A1

Similar to M3 series in suspension: twin Cadillac engines with hydramatic shift. The maximum speed of light tanks is 40 miles per hour. Equipped with dual controls.

WEIGHT:_____ ARMAMENT:_____
MI. PER GAL:_____ FRONT ARMOR:_____

# MEDIUM TANKS

Medium tanks are used for heavy combat and as a "striking force." They weigh between 28 and 32 tons, depending on power plant and armament. They can be powered by a 9 cyl. aircraft-type engine, twin Diesels, V8 special tank engine or a "multi-bank" power plant. These engines deliver approximately 1 mile per gallon.

Principal armament: 75 mm gun equipped with stabilizer; 50 cal. machine guns used as antiaircraft.

### MEDIUM TANK M4 SERIES

HULL:_____ENGINE, M4A2:_____M4A3:___
CREW:_____WEIGHT:_____SPEED:_____MPH

Characteristics: Low silhouette, 75mm gun in turret, 360 degree traverse, rounded hull, greater vision for driver, greater maximum speed.

Other models: M4A1 (Wright engine) M4A4 (Chrysler engine).

LIGHT TANK T9E1

LIGHT TANK M3A3

LIGHT TANK M5A1

MEDIUM TANK M4A3

# SPECIAL PURPOSE VEHICLES

HEAVY WRECKER, M1 ("10-Ton Wrecker")

Highly specialized vehicle; operates efficiently under all conditions; used for medium weight vehicle-recovery and lifting of heavy objects such as tank engines, gun tubes, etc. Carries equipment for towing, repairing and salvaging, (tow bar, tackle, anchors, spades; welding, cutting and hand tools).

WEIGHT:_____ ENGINE:_____ H.P.:_____

LENGTH:_____GAS CAP:_____SPEED:_____MPH

WINCH CAPACITIES (single line), FRONT:_____

REAR: _____ BOOM:_____

MEDIUM WRECKER, (4 Ton Diamond-T)

This wrecker is similarly employed for lighter work. It is smaller, has only three winches. It has two booms, each with its winch and jack. With a boom to the side position, traffic can pass under the line while a job is being done on that side.

WEIGHT:_____ ENGINE:_____ H.P._____

LENGTH:_____GAS CAP:_____ SPEED:____MPH.

WINCH CAPACITIES (Single line), FRONT:_____

BOOM WINCHES:_____

TRUCK, BOMB SERVICE, M6

1-purpose vehicle developed by the Ordnance Dept. for the Air Force. Used to tow bomb trailers and to facilitate loading bombs into aircraft bomb racks.

WEIGHT:_____ ENGINE: _____ H.P.____

CREW:_____ GAS CAP:____ SPEED:___MPH.

WINCH CAPACITY:_____

TRACTOR, MEDIUM, M6

This tractor is a specialized vehicle for towing heavy artillery over rough terrain. Equipped with twin engines developing a total of 430 H.P.

WEIGHT:_____ ENGINE: _____ H.P._____

CREW:_____GAS CAP:____SPEED:___MPH.

WINCH CAPACITY:_____

# MOTOR VEHICLE OPERATION

The life of every soldier may depend upon his ability to operate a motor vehicle. For this reason every Ordnance Soldier must learn the fundamentals of vehicle operation and care.

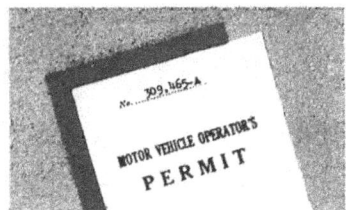
THE MOTOR VEHICLE OPERATOR'S PERMIT
Is evidence of the person's ability to operate an Army vehicle.

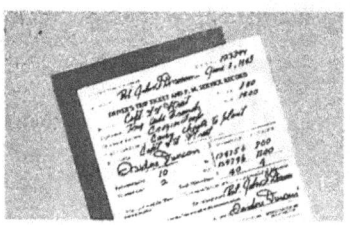
THE TRIP TICKET
Is authority to use an Army vehicle for a specific purpose at a specific time.

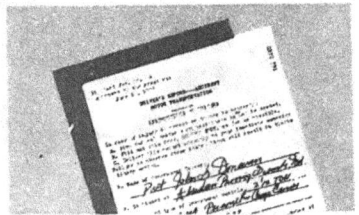
THE ACCIDENT REPORT
Must always be in the vehicle. In case of accident fill it out "on the spot".

THE 3 FORMS ABOVE MUST BE IN DRIVER'S POSSESSION WHEN OPERATING AN ARMY VEHICLE.

## SAFETY FIRST!
You are responsible for the safe operation and proper care of your vehicle at all times.

KEEP TO THE RIGHT

DON'T PASS ON HILLS

STOP AT UNGUARDED RAILROADS

NEVER OVERLOAD

CHECK CARGO FREQUENTLY

SQUARE SIGNS mean Caution.

DIAMOND SIGNS mean Reduce Speed.

OCTAGONAL SIGNS mean Stop.

ROUND SIGNS mean Railroad Crossings

RIGHT TURN

LEFT TURN

STOP OR SLOW

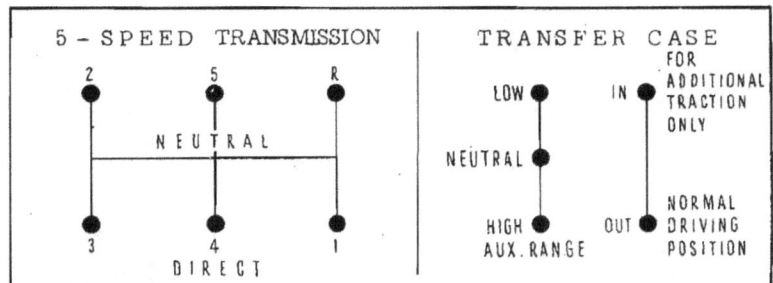 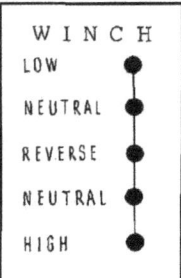

(Diagram for 2 1/2 ton Truck)

A diagram similar to the above will be found on instrument panel of every vehicle.
This locates lever positions for transmissions, transfer case, and front wheel drive.

For movement over difficult terrain, many army vehicles are equipped with a winch. Diagrams of the above type indicate positions of the winch control lever.

## MAINTENANCE

First Echelon Maintenance is preventive maintenance. The driver is responsible for constant inspection and regular servicing of the vehicle to prevent damage during operation. No vehicle should be operated unless it is in proper condition. Never attempt repairs unless you have the proper tools and know how to make the repairs. The driver must see that the vehicle is always ready for use.

The driver must inspect his vehicle before operation, while driving, at a halt, and after operation. Some of the more important checks are:

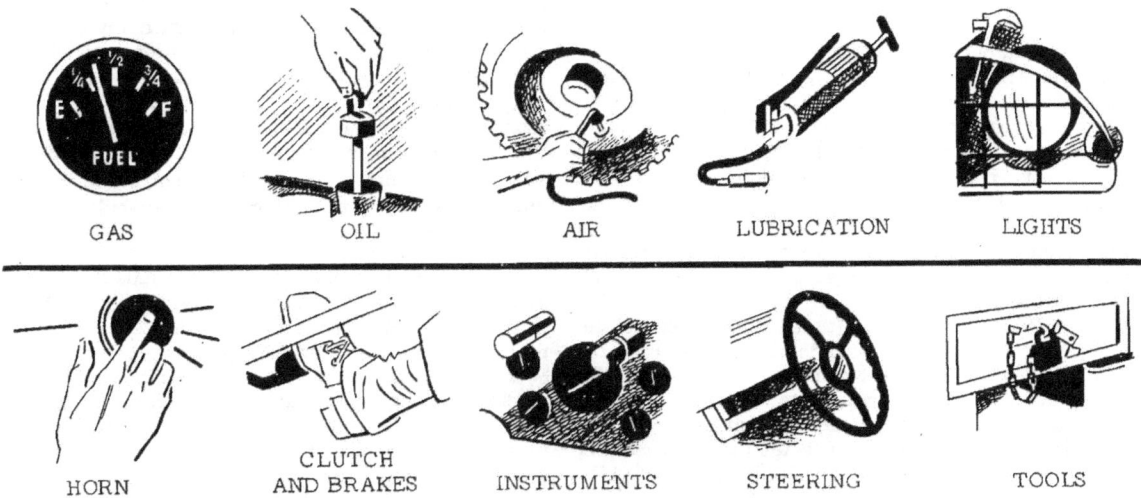

GAS    OIL    AIR    LUBRICATION    LIGHTS

HORN    CLUTCH AND BRAKES    INSTRUMENTS    STEERING    TOOLS

# CLERKS

THERE ARE TWO BROAD CATEGORIES
OF ORDNANCE CLERKS:

GENERAL CLERKS
(Administrative and Personnel)

SUPPLY CLERKS
(Dealing principally with Ammunition Supply
and Ordnance General Supply)

## GENERAL CLERKS

The responsibility of the General Clerk in the Ordnance Department is to reflect correctly in his paper work the operation of his organization. Behind every record, especially a personnel record, is a man whose rights are vitally related to that record. Ninety percent of army work is administration, and less than ten percent is fighting.

Let us consider the steps in the military career of a typical soldier and the necessary clerical details and records connected with him. At the Reception Center, the SERVICE RECORD is initiated to keep a complete history of his service from the date of entry until discharge, death, or retirement. Included herein are records of Sex Morality lectures, Articles of War lectures, Vaccinations and Immunizations. The man's skills and aptitudes are tested by classification, examinations, and interviews. His degrees of skill in various fields are described by a specification serial number which is identified by a coded symbol (number) punched in the SOLDIER'S QUALIFICATION CARD. During his service this card must be kept up to date as to military specialties, schools attended, promotions, transfers and other items which will indicate his particular field of usefulness.

The man will be sent to a company for basic training via a SPECIAL ORDER. In this organization, PAY ROLLS, MORNING REPORTS (daily history of the company), DAILY SICK REPORTS, DUTY ROSTERS, and various company reports pertaining to supply and property, company mess, and company funds will be prepared.

These are only a few of the records and forms that general clerks handle or prepare. In order to insure coordination in all the echelons of the army the clerk must be trained in the use of publications such as Army Regulations, War Department Circulars, General Orders, Bulletins, Field Manuals, Technical Manuals, etc. He must know the basic principles of his job. An understanding of the over-all scheme will enable him to realize that army methods and administrative organizations are generally simple and clear-cut.

The army is the country's largest industry, comprising several million men working under one head. It is world-wide, operating on land, on sea, and in the air. It administers its personnel twenty-four hours a day and provides food, clothing, housing, medical attention, amusements, spiritual supervision, and — it must fight. The role of the clerk, in accurately recording and reporting on the foregoing, contributes immeasureably to orderly processes and unimpaired morale of the men so that training and functioning may proceed unhampered.

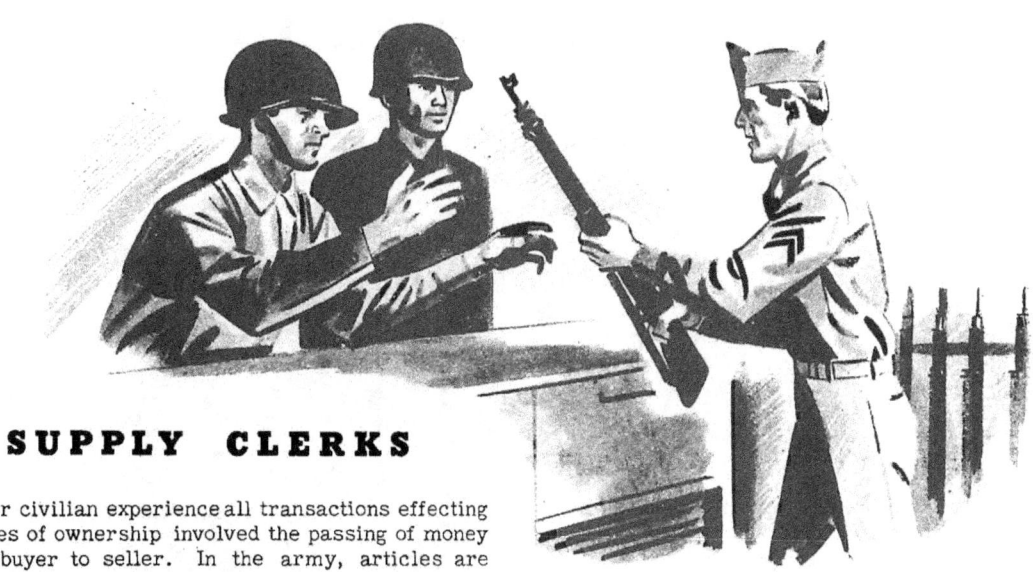

# SUPPLY CLERKS

In your civilian experience all transactions effecting changes of ownership involved the passing of money from buyer to seller. In the army, articles are issued and pass from hand to hand by change of accountability and responsibility. In broad terms, accountability is the obligation to keep complete and accurate records of property. Responsibility is personal financial liability for property. In the army, no one gains complete ownership of a government issued article.

The importance of the paper work that a clerk may have to perform becomes apparent when you learn that the Ordnance Department issues about 400,000 different items to the various branches of the army.

For example, Joe Smith - your brother, your friend, or your neighbor - is in an active theater of war as a part of an Infantry unit. During the course of the fighting, his rifle becomes damaged beyond repair. He is issued a new one with no questions asked. What is the supply system that made this immediate issue possible?

Let us trace, from its origin, this rifle and the paper work necessary to get it to Joe when he needs it. An arsenal in the United States manufactured the rifle. Until it is issued, proper records must be kept, charging the arsenal with its possession. This record is the STOCK RECORD ACCOUNT and indicates stock balances and quantities due in and due out.

Joe's unit will carry a surplus of reserve items in anticipation of loss or damage. These articles will be procured from a supply organization in the field called an Ordnance Depot. Depots stock items for many units like Joe's and maintain authorized levels by procuring and replenishing, in turn, from the arsenal.

"Here you are, keep it clean."

When depot stock levels fall, a formal request from the depot to the arsenal, called a REQUISITION, causes supplies to flow forward. The arsenal assembles and issues all articles listed on the requisition. To show this issue on its stock record account, the arsenal prepares a SHIPPING TICKET, which transfers accountability and responsibility to the depot. This will also be the means by which the depot will pick up possession of the articles on its stock record account.

Now Joe's organization will requisition on the depot for its authorized rifles. The depot doesn't act merely as a middle-man. It has removed obstacles of time, distance, transportation, and preservation. Joe's unit will get its rifles when it needs them.

The transfer of the rifles from the arsenal to the Infantry unit will be completed when the latter organization picks them up on its records with a corresponding change in the records of the depot. A shipping ticket will again be used to show these changes.

The flow of articles will not always be as smooth as has been indicated here. Difficulties will arise which must be adjusted by additional paper work. Therefore, you can see that the clerk has an important job - one that must be well done if all the Joes in the army are to get what they need when they need it.

# SOURCES OF INFORMATION

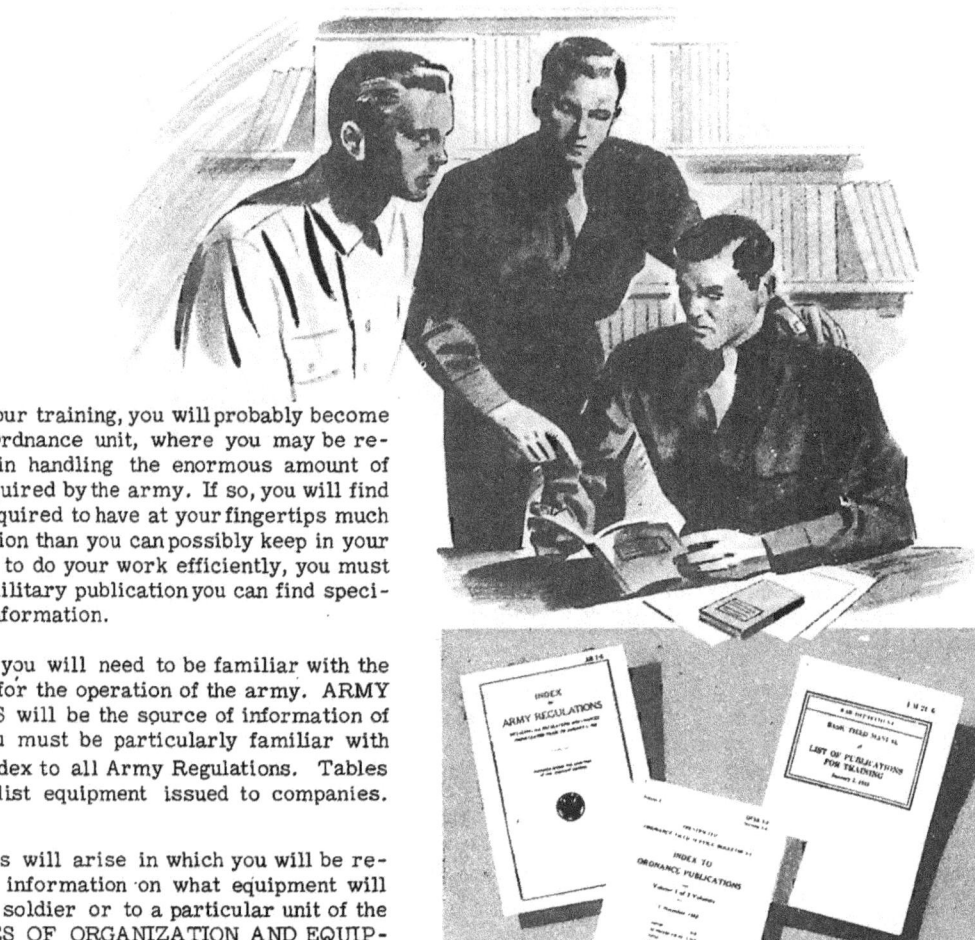

At the end of your training, you will probably become a part of an Ordnance unit, where you may be required to aid in handling the enormous amount of paper work required by the army. If so, you will find that you are required to have at your fingertips much more information than you can possibly keep in your head. In order to do your work efficiently, you must know in what military publication you can find specified kinds of information.

For example, you will need to be familiar with the general rules for the operation of the army. ARMY REGULATIONS will be the source of information of this kind. You must be particularly familiar with AR 1-5, the index to all Army Regulations. Tables of Equipment list equipment issued to companies.

Many occasions will arise in which you will be required to give information on what equipment will be issued to a soldier or to a particular unit of the army. TABLES OF ORGANIZATION AND EQUIPMENT will supply the number, qualifications, and duties of all enlisted men in a unit and also the major items of equipment. TABLES OF ALLOWANCES will show the allowances of such items as beds, desks, and other items which troops do not take with them when they go into the field. TABLES OF BASIC ALLOWANCES, prepared for an entire arm or service, show all equipment taken into the field.

You will need to be familiar with the various field manuals in order to supply your unit with such information as it may require. FIELD MANUALS are reference books concerned with military training and field operations. More detailed explanations are contained in TECHNICAL MANUALS, used by instructors and specialists. Both these publications are indexed in FM 21-6.

There are many other general publications with which you must be familiar. WAR DEPARTMENT BULLETINS and CIRCULARS are constantly being published, giving information about many phases of the army. You will need to make frequent references to these publications and make variations in your work to conform with them.

The publications named above are general in nature. In addition to these, many special pamphlets are published by the Ordnance Department, which are of interest only to the Ordnance soldier. You will need to be particularly familiar with all these publications.

ORDNANCE FIELD SERVICE BULLETINS (new issues are published as War Department Bulletins) are illustrative of these pamphlets. Here you will find administrative and supply information of interest to Ordnance field units. Such subjects as how to care for unsafe ammunition and lubrication of all types of Ordnance vehicles will be found here.

OFSB 1-1 is the index of all Ordnance publications published as of 1 Jan 1944. However, all of the Ordnance Field Service publications are being converted to War Department publications and will be indexed in FM 21-6, List of Publications for Training, and changes thereto. For some time it will be necessary for Ordnance units to use both OFSB 1-1 and FM 21-6. Later when such an index becomes necessary, Ordnance Field Service publications (current at that date and not converted into War Department publications) will be indexed in War Department Supply Bulletin (SB), 9-1.

STANDARD NOMENCLATURE LISTS, the Sears-Roebuck catalog of the Ordnance Department, are used for all requisitioning of Ordnance materiel. These lists give the proper nomenclature and stock numbers of Ordnance items, and also include pictures, prices, and allowances of these items. Major items of equipment and spare parts are arranged in groups according to the type of article and are listed alphabetically. The index to these lists is the ORDNANCE PUBLICATIONS FOR SUPPLY INDEX, which provides a quick and accurate method of determining the specific Standard Nomenclature List required. The OPSI is issued as Army Service Forces Catalog, Ord. 2.

Four other important publications should be mentioned. ORDNANCE STORAGE AND SHIPMENT CHARTS give all necessary data for storage and shipment of Ordnance materiel. Such data as type of container, weight of item, and number of containers per carload are included. ORDNANCE EQUIPMENT CHARTS list all Ordnance equipment carried by a unit of the army and are an excellent source for determining what items of equipment must be serviced by a maintenance unit. ORDNANCE FIELD SERVICE TECHNICAL BULLETINS (or W.D. Technical Bulletins) are widely used in the field.

They supply new technical information in advance of publication of technical manuals, making possible rapid changes in equipment and maintenance. FIELD SERVICE MODIFICATION WORK ORDERS are used for a somewhat similar purpose. These publications permit some changes in Ordnance equipment to be made in the field and direct that others be made in the arsenals.

These are the most important publications you, as a soldier in an Ordnance unit, will need to use as references. Many others, more specialized in nature, will also be used from time to time. You should be especially familiar with the indexes to all these publications, since speed and accuracy are of paramount importance.

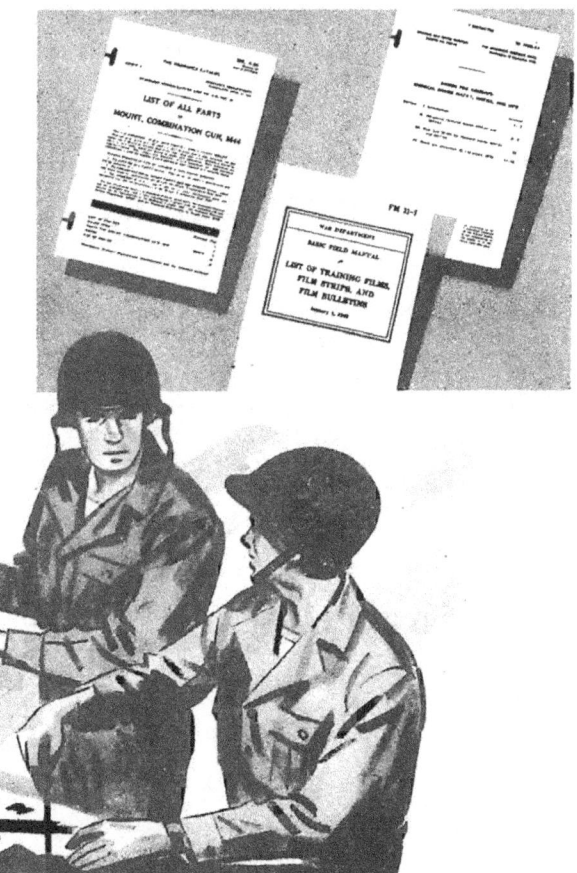

# FIRE CONTROL INSTRUMENTS

Fire Control equipment includes all instruments used to control and give correction to the fire of guns. Instruments are divided into two general classifications:

A. Fire Control Instruments (Off-carriage) - not mounted on gun
B. Sighting Equipment (On-carriage) - mounted on the gun

## OFF-CARRIAGE INSTRUMENTS

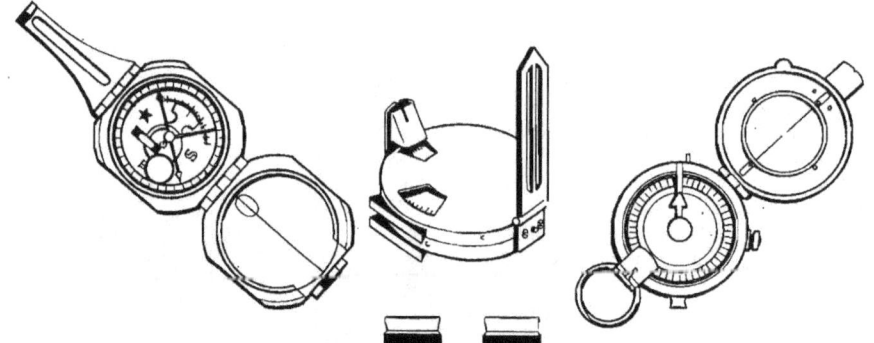

### 1. BINOCULARS

Used for observation and correction of fire. Two telescopes are hinged together to aid in depth perception.

The left telescope contains a reticle (a scale seen when looking through the instrument) used to measure small horizontal and vertical angles. Each telescope focuses to suit observer's eyes.

### 2. COMPASSES

Multiple purpose instruments used by all branches of the service, primarily for measuring angles of magnetic azimuth (a clockwise angle from magnetic north). Front and rear sights are provided for sighting accurately on targets. Certain types have either a magnifying prism or lens to facilitate reading the scale.

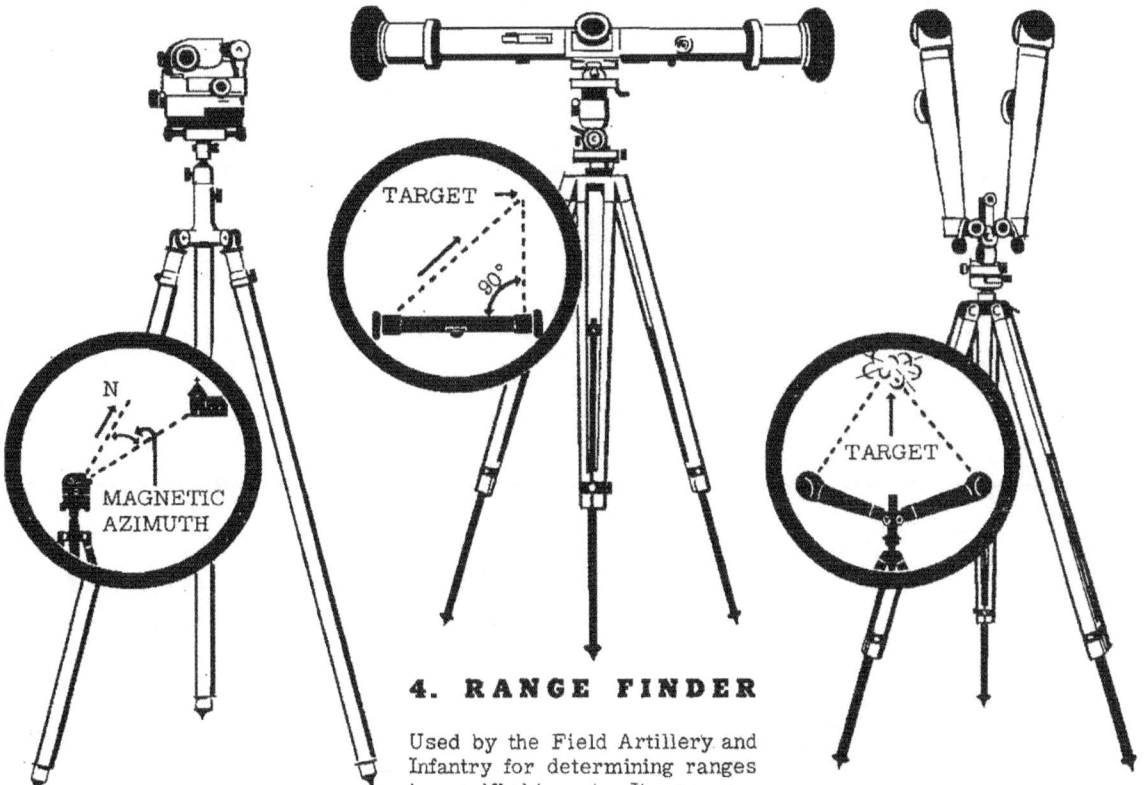

## 3. AIMING CIRCLE

Used by the Field Artillery for the purpose of computing and applying firing data. It is composed of a small focusing telescope and a compass mounted on a tripod.

It is used to measure angles of magnetic azimuth, firing angles, and for survey work.

## 4. RANGE FINDER

Used by the Field Artillery and Infantry for determining ranges to specified targets. It measures ranges from 400 to 20,000 yards by means of triangulation, using the length of the instrument as the base of the triangle. The right window of the instrument is placed in direct line with the target, forming a 90° angle with the base. A movable lens in the left side of the instrument determines the other angle and automatically computes the range, which is read from the range scale.

## 5. BATTERY COMMANDER'S TELESCOPE

Used by the Field Artillery for the observation and correction of fire. Consists of two periscopic type telescopes hinged together and mounted on a tripod. Right telescope contains a reticle used to measure necessary corrections, based upon the observation of shell bursts.

## 6. GUNNER'S QUADRANT

Used by the Field Artillery for setting a weapon in elevation. A level is mounted on a movable arm, which can be set on its frame for any desired elevation angle. The instrument is also used to level the gun carriage.

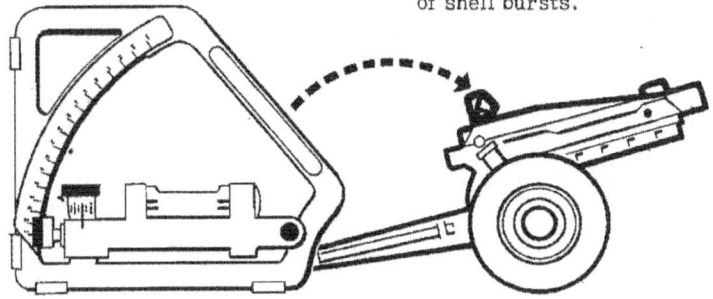

# ON-CARRIAGE INSTRUMENTS

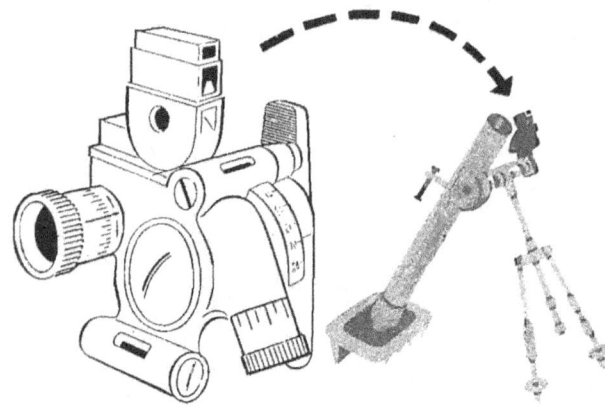

### 7. MORTAR SIGHT

The Mortar Sight is a non-optical instrument latched in place on the left side of the 60mm or 81mm mortar. An open sight (similar to the sight on the Springfield rifle) is used for aiming the mortar, and a level provides a datum line for elevation settings.

In operation, an aiming stake is placed in line with the mortar and target as a reference point for the open sight. Elevation settings are made on the scales provided, and the mortar is elevated until the level is centered.

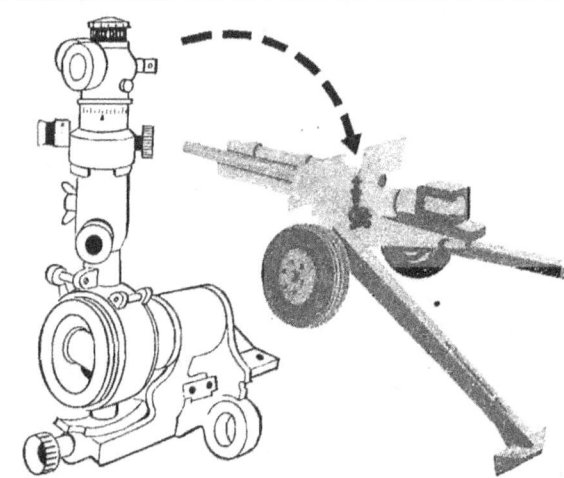

### 8. TELESCOPE MOUNT AND PANORAMIC TELESCOPE

The instruments on the left side of a gun or howitzer are employed to aim the weapon in azimuth (to the right or left). The Telescope Mount, affixed to the gun and moving with it, holds the Panoramic Telescope.

The Panoramic Telescope is so constructed that its head can be rotated throughout a complete circle, and thus the gunner can place the aiming stake at any convenient spot. The azimuth scale on the Telescope is used in applying corrections to the fire of the weapon.

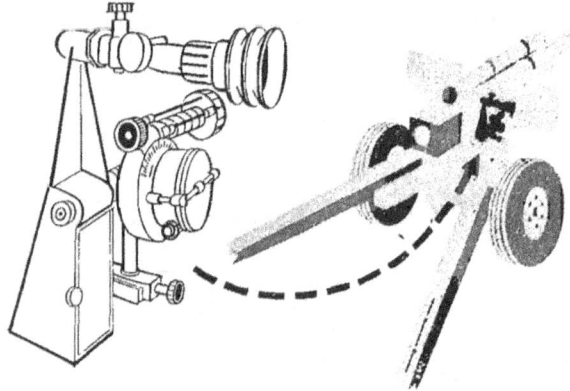

### 9. RANGE QUADRANT AND ELBOW TELESCOPE

The instruments on the right side of the gun are used to set the weapon to the specified elevation. The Elbow Telescope and the Range Quadrant are used independently of each other.

The Elbow Telescope is used when the target is directly visible (a tank). The Range Quadrant is used when firing indirectly (on a distant target). In operation, the necessary settings are made on the scales of the Range Quadrant and the gun is elevated until the level is centered.

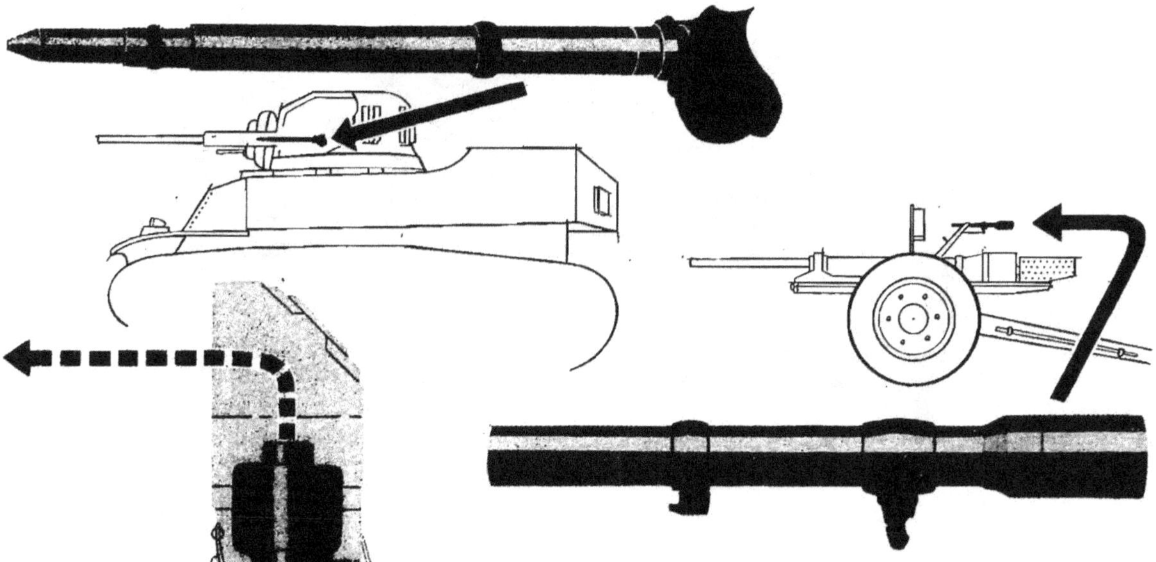

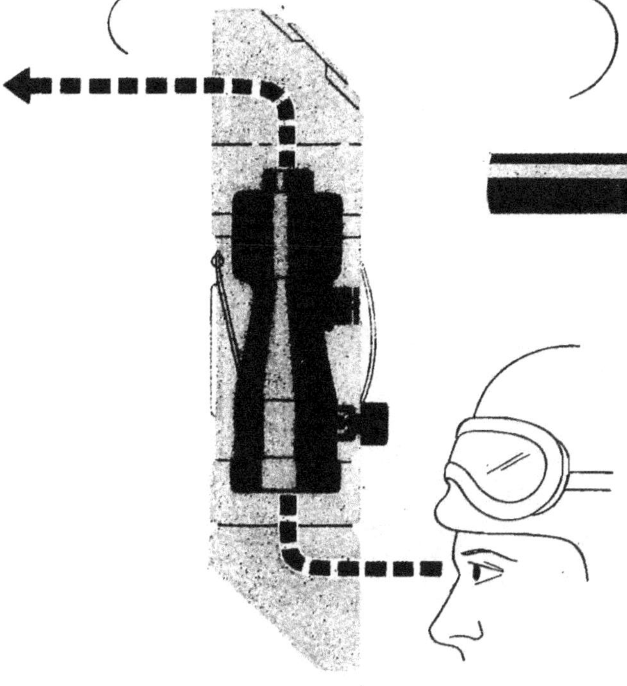

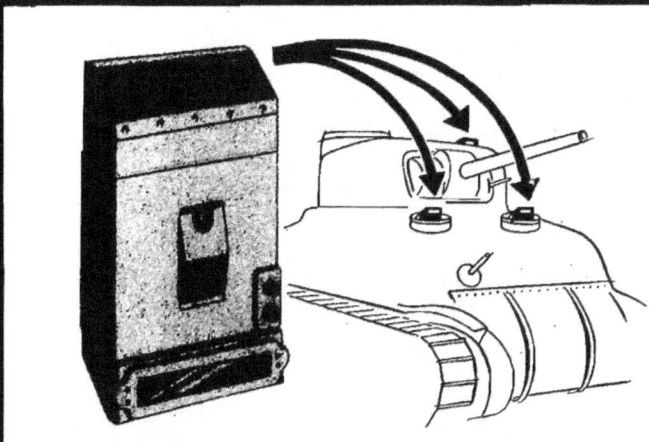

## 10. TELESCOPES

Straight Telescopes are used as direct-sighting equipment for tank guns and anti-tank guns. Each Straight Telescope is made up of a system of lenses so arranged and adjusted as to give the observer a distinct and enlarged view of the target. Each Telescope is mounted parallel to and moves with the gun tube. Therefore, by sighting the Telescope correctly at the target, the fire of the gun will be accurate.

## 11. PERISCOPES

Tank crews are able to observe the target through periscopes without exposing themselves to enemy fire.

Aiming periscopes contain within the periscope body a small straight telescope between two mirrors. Observation periscopes contain the mirrors without the small telescope.

# SHOP TRUCKS

TRUCK, ORDNANCE MAINTENANCE

## MEDIUM MAINTENANCE EQUIPMENT

The Ordnance Department has made tremendous advancements in the current war in the development of shop maintenance trucks and equipment for the use of Ordnance maintenance units in the field.

Present shop trucks include the most modern and complete equipment. Provisions are made for blackout and air-conditioning of the trucks so that work can proceed at night or during gas attack.

●

MEDIUM MAINTENANCE SHOP EQUIPMENT: An Ordnance Medium Maintenance Company is ordinarily equipped with the following shop trucks and equipment:

1. Artillery Repair Truck.
2. Automotive Repair Truck.
3. Electrical Repair Truck.
4. Instrument Repair Truck.
5. Machine Shop Truck, Load "A".
6. Small Arms Repair Trucks.
7. Welding Truck.
8. 3rd Echelon Set No. 1.
9. Special Tool Sets.

# CONTENTS OF TRUCKS

ARTILLERY REPAIR TRUCK

a. Rigging Equipment.
b. Portable Electric Drill.
c. Artillery Mechanics' Tool Kit and Assorted hand tools.

AUTOMOTIVE REPAIR TRUCK

a. Portable Electric Drill
b. 10-ton Press (Porto-Power)
c. Valve Spring Tester
d. Valve refacing and reseating tools.
e. Lubricating guns and equipment
f. Automotive repair tool kits
g. Special engine tool and accessories.

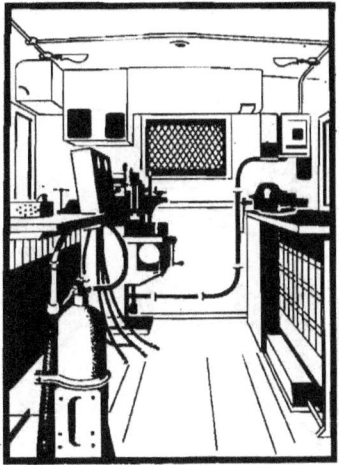

ELECTRICAL REPAIR TRUCK

a. Distributor Tester
b. Condenser Tester
c. Battery Charger (Portable)
d. Engine Test Analyzer
e. Automotive Mechanics Tool Kit
f. Electrical Test bench

INSTRUMENT REPAIR TRUCK

(a.) Portable Electric Drill (b.) Bench Drill Press (c.) Bench Grinder (d.) 10" Metal Turning Lathe (e.) Precision Measuring Instruments (f.) Threading sets, drills, etc. (g.) Instrument repair tool kits and supplies (h.) Leather worker's kit.

MACHINE SHOP TRUCK, LOAD "A"

(a.) 7" Bench Shaper (b.) Sensitive Drill Press (c.) Portable Electric Drills (d.) Bench Grinder (e.) 10-ton Hydraulic Press (f.) 10" Bench Lathe (Sheldon) (g.) Precision Measuring Instruments. (h.) Taps, dies, drills, reamer, milling cutters, etc. (i.) General hand tools.

# CONTENTS OF TRUCKS

SMALL ARMS REPAIR TRUCK

### SMALL ARMS REPAIR TRUCK
a. Portable Electric Drill.
b. 1 1/2 KW Gasoline Generator.
c. Bench Grinder.
d. Armorer's Tool kit.
e. Precision Small Arms Gauges.

### WELDING TRUCK
a. Portable Electric Drill.
b. Power Hack Saw.
c. Portable Grinder.
d. Arc Welding Equipment.
e. Oxy-Acetylene Welding and Cutting Equipment.
f. Welding Electrodes and supplies.
g. Welder's tool kit.
h. Blacksmith forge and tools.

WELDING TRUCK

## THIRD ECHELON SET, NO. 1

a. Spray painting equipment.
b. Blacksmith's tools and forge.
c. Lubrication guns and equipment.
d. Air Compressor.
e. Battery Charger.
f. Bench Grinders.
g. 3000 Watt Gasoline Generator.
h. Automotive electrical testing equipment.
i. Oxy-Acetylene Welding equipment.
j. Precision measuring tools.
k. Special automotive tools.
l. General hand tools.

## SPECIAL TOOL SETS

a. Battery Expert's.
b. Blacksmith's.
c. Body Mechanic's.
d. Electrical and Carburetor Mechanic's.
e. Machinist's.
f. Motor Vehicle Mechanic's.
g. Painter's.
h. Sheet Metal and Radiator Mechanic's.
i. Canvas Worker's.
j. Carpenter's.

# UNIFORM IDENTIFICATION

THE VETERAN BRITISH TOMMY...

His winter uniform (above) consists of brown windbreaker-type blouse and long trousers. In place of leggings he wears gaiters. His equipment includes deep ammunition pouches, knapsack, canteen, raincape, gas mask, entrenching tool and bayonet. Note the large inverted chevrons.

For dress, the dashing beret replaces his "tin hat", and in summer he wears a khaki uniform of shirt and shorts.

● AND OUR FRIEND, THE MIGHTY RUSSIAN

His helmet is more conical than ours. In summer he wears a flaring slipover blouse of O.D. buttoned at the cuffs, and O.D. breeches tucked into high black boots. (Figure at near right.) The ammunition pouches on his belt resemble the German's.

In winter his uniform is of quilted O.D. cloth, tan felt boots which look like heavy stockings, and fur cap with ear flaps. Note the collar patches and Red Star insignia on cap. (Figure at extreme right.)

# THE ONLY GOOD JAP...

...is a dead Jap. He is plenty tough and can hike 35 miles every day for a week. He knows how to fight dirty, is good at sneaking through jungles and likes to flank your position and fire on you from the rear.

His uniform is often improvised. Regular dress, shown at far left, is khaki or khaki-green, and his pack resembles the German's. In jungle warfare he wears only shirts, shorts and sneakers. To deceive you he may wear anything — native clothing, British uniforms, etc. To blend himself with his surroundings he puts leaves in his helmet and branches in his belt, or he may wear a jungle jacket of fibre like the wounded Jap above.

P.S. Don't trust a Jap, wounded or otherwise. Keep him covered from a short distance while another man disarms him and searches him thoroughly.

# THIS IS THE NAZI ... SHOOT TO KILL!

Shoot the parachutist in the air — while he's helpless. Learn to spot these details of his uniform: Round helmet with short lip and harness-type headstrap; coverall which may be discarded in combat; blue-gray blouse worn under the coverall and matching trousers tucked into side-laced boots.

The German infantryman, shown at right, wears the coal scuttle-shaped helmet, gray-green blouse and trousers and high boots. Note the shoulder straps, collar patches and chevrons (on left sleeve only).

His equipment includes leather cartridge clip pouches worn on belt (front view), gas mask in metal cylinder, shelter half, canteen, mess kit, respirator, gas cape, haversack and entrenching tool (rear view).

Like the Jap, he's tough — if anything, better trained. When you meet up with him in the field, you think of him more as a cog in a big machine than as an individual. So learn to recognize his machines, too... especially tanks, armored cars, trucks and planes.

# TIPS FROM AN OLD TOP KICK

Perhaps your duty will carry you to England. If so, you'll be given a book when you get on the boat — a book designed to help you get along with our Allies. We can give you a few tips now, though.

Remember that when you're in England, you'll be a guest. Don't be impolite.

Don't tell the English we won the last war for them. We didn't. We helped to win it, and so did they — but they lost 16 times as many men as we did.

You'll probably find England a bit different from what you expected. You'll find many of the houses unpainted, because the British have things to make which are more important than paint. You'll find many buildings grimy — because Englishmen have been a little too busy to wash them.

And speaking of Englishmen, they'll seem a bit reserved, judging by American standards. A typical Briton won't speak to you unless you speak to him first. That doesn't mean he isn't interested; it's a British custom of respecting the other fellow's privacy.

You're in the best-paid Army in the world, but don't flaunt your roll. The British Tommies don't like to be constantly reminded that they're not as well paid as we are.

Don't make a play for a Tommy's girl. She may like it but he won't. You may become involved in a physical discussion and get thrown in the pokey. Of course, if you can find a single, unattached girl, more power to you. You'll probably acquire some English slang, too. Just remember when and where to use it. "Bloody", for example, should never be used in front of a girl — it's a low-down cussword. In Brooklyn, a "bum" is a Dodger. In England, it means somebody's back side.

You'll learn as you go along. Just remember, it's impolite to criticize your hosts. It's militarily stupid to criticize your Allies.

Guardsman Patrick Tivey of the British Coldstream Guards passes a word to the wise from his station in Libya. Writing for the American Magazine, he says that water's scarce in the desert, so if you want hot water for shaving, drain some from a truck radiator. It's a little rusty, but you're not going to drink it. And when you've finished, pour it back into the radiator again.

You can heat your canned emergency rations with a truck. Just wire the can around the exhaust manifold. Then, when you stop for chow, dinner's hot. Don't make a cooking fire unless you have to — but if you must, take a 5-gallon gasoline can, shovel in 6 or 8 inches of sand and about a quart of gasoline, and light it. The sand acts like a wick.

Plenty of men in Libya died because they were too lazy to dig a slit trench. Look at page 36 to see how it's done. Remember, not too deep, or it might cave in. Just get below ground level.

In addition to what Guardsman Tivey says, here are a few extra tips. In the desert, you must discipline yourself in the use of water. Get the habit of drinking very little during the day. It's especially tough to do this if you smoke a great deal, so you'd better cut down on cigarettes, too.

At all times in the desert you should wear a "belly band" to prevent stomach chills. This is necessary even on the hottest days. If your girl likes to knit sweaters, there's your answer.

If you wind up in jungle country, get yourself a pocket knife before you go into the interior. It's apt to be your most valued possession. Carry your matches in a special waterproof container. Otherwise, perspiration alone will ruin them. Always sleep under a mosquito net. In the rainy season, and at other times if possible, sleep off the ground. You and your buddy, if using a pup tent, can build a little platform of forked twigs and branches, <u>at least a foot off the ground</u>, lashing the parts together with vines. Pitch shelter tent and mosquito netting on the platform.

Avoid brushing against trees and bushes wherever possible, since many are poisonous.

If you're unlucky enough to be bitten by a jungle snake, don't run. Kill the snake if possible, as identification is an aid to medical treatment. Apply a tourniquet, if you're bitten on an arm or leg, and send your buddy for a medical officer immediately.

If you should get lost, remember these points. Streams and water courses are usually found if you go down hill, and these sooner or later will lead to inhabited regions. A light improvised spear with barbed points will enable you to kill fish. Edible fruits can usually be identified by signs of animals having eaten them. Avoid eating unknown fruits, except in an extreme emergency.

Remember that if you keep relaxed and use your head, you can live and travel alone for weeks in the jungle.

When you're on duty in cold climates, one of the dangers you'll face will be freezing and frostbite. Freezing is not always accompanied by pain. It is indicated by a grayish or whitish appearance of the skin. It's a good idea to wrinkle the face from time to time to discover any stiffness caused by freezing. If a part of your face seems stiff, you can thaw it by placing your bare hand over the area until circulation is restored.

Don't wear a beard. Frost from the breath accumulates on the whiskers, and you'll wind up with a frozen pan. Either shave frequently, using an oily shaving cream, or keep the beard closely trimmed with clippers.

You'll have to wear snow glasses during the daytime to prevent snow-blindness. In an emergency, you can blacken the skin around your eyes, just like an outfielder on a ball club.

If you have to wade across shallow streams or overflows in regions of extreme cold with shoes that are not waterproof, try this: Dip the shoes into the water and withdraw them quickly. A thin coating of ice will form. Then you can wade quickly across, and after a few minutes, the ice will crack off your shoes. It's an old Eskimo trick.

Speaking of shoes, its a good idea to stuff dried grass around your feet, inside the shoes. The grass absorbs moisture and should be changed daily. Also, dried grass held in the hands will help retain heat.

No matter where you go in the service of your country, you're a part of the best-clothed, best-equipped and best-paid army in the world. That doesn't make it the best army in the world — because only you can do that. From now on it's up to you.

# THE WAR: *HOW IT STARTED!*

## IN JAPAN

**1875** A gang of hard-boiled generals and admirals in Japan exercised power in the name of the Emperor, who, they taught the people, was heaven-born. With a god as their leader they were convinced they would eventually conquer the world. They resented the economic advancement of the United States and Britain in the Far East and planned to wage a great war against them. Seizing the Kurile Islands to the north, the Japanese made their first attempt to expand. Other Pacific islands were occupied.

**1895** Japan, made up of only four small islands, was in itself incapable of developing into a great industrial nation. To fulfill what they termed their "divine destiny" the war lords realized they had to conquer China first. In a brief war with this backward country they were victorious and took Formosa and the Pescadores.

**1905** The Japanese plan for a war had always begun with a "sneak" attack. In this way they sank the Russian Asiatic fleet and gained Karafuto. They occupied the peninsula of Korea, extending from China into the Sea of Japan.

**1919** In order to gain Germany's colonial islands in the Pacific, Japan was an Ally in the World War but did practically no fighting. The League of Nations gave Japan the Marshall, Caroline, and Marianas Islands under a mandate which provided that they remain unfortified. Almost immediately the Japanese violated this provision.

**1931** Having potential bases scattered throughout the Pacific and Korea as a foothold in Asia, Japan turned actively toward carving out a large continental Empire. Using the pretext of an "incident" and the false need of maintaining order, the Japanese launched a bold program of aggression by invading Manchuria. They overran the entire province in one year, gaining vast amounts of materials vital in waging war.

**1932** The Japanese, seeking to encircle China, took the city of Shanghai which gave them a base for operations directed at the heart of the country.

**1937** Finally, the Japanese were ready to begin absorbing China, and struck southward from Manchuria where they had installed a puppet Government. They discovered, however, that against stubborn Chinese resistance the small part of the war machine they were willing to use had to alter its strategy. Later, from Shanghai, as an alternative plan, they began their policy of creeping down the coast to seize the sea ports and strangle China. Meanwhile, the larger part of the Japanese military forces were being trained in Manchuria and the home islands.

**1940** Japan made a treaty with Germany and Italy who recognized "her leadership in Greater East Asia." Actually what Hitler, Mussolini, and Japan had done was apportion the world for attack. While the two European dictators were to have dominion over Europe and Africa, Japan was to be supreme in East Asia.

**1940** After France fell, Japan occupied Indo-China for its resources and strategic position close to the Burma Road, China's lifeline for supplies, and also near the British naval base at Singapore.

**1941** The United States was disturbed by the developments in Japan and aided China with money and supplies, at the same time stopping all exports of iron and gasoline to Japan. The United States entered into negotiations with the Japanese in an attempt to persuade them to give up their program of aggression.

**1941** On December 7, while the Japanese envoys were still conversing with our State Department, Japan struck, furiously bombing Pearl Harbor. Eighty-six ships of the Pacific fleet and most of our aircraft were disabled there. Three hours later Japan declared war on the United States.

**1941** Seventy-two hours after the attack on Pearl Harbor, Japan invaded the Philippines. Under General Douglas MacArthur American and Filipino troops waged an heroic battle on the peninsula of Bataan. With our fleet crippled, we were unable to send either reinforcements or supplies, however, it took the Japanese four months to end resistance.

**1941** The enemy seized our naval bases and air stations at Guam and Wake and so, almost without interference, Japan marched into a tremendous empire within three months. Singapore and Hong Kong fell. Burma and the Netherlands East Indies were invaded. With these conquests Japan had come into possession of the world's most important sources of rubber, tin, and quinine.

# IN GERMANY

**1933** Adolf Hitler, an enemy of democratic liberties, became German Chancellor, January 30. With an army that the militarists had been planning since 1919, he was determined to make Germany the dominant state in the world. He had already convinced most Germans that they belonged to a "Master Race" and had the right to rule the rest of humanity.

**1935** The world learned that Germany was building submarines and had begun forced military service.

**1936** On November 25, Germany and Japan signed the Anti-Comintern Pact, pledging joint action against the ideas of Soviet Russia. This was part of Hitler's smokescreen to deceive the Democracies into believing that he had no ambitions against them.

**1936** To test their armies as well as extend fascist influence to Spain, Germany and Mussolini's Italy sent 220,000 troops to fight the Republican Government which was trying to put down an anti-democratic revolt.

**1938** After German armed threats had terrified the Austrian Government and Nazi propaganda confused the Austrian people, Hitler ordered his army across the frontier. Seven million Austrians became German subjects. In this way Hitler was strengthening himself for his war against the world.

**1938** At Munich in September, Britain and France, who were trying to prevent war, gave Hitler the western rim of democratic Czechoslovakia. Less than a year later he took the rest of the country. This proved to be his last "bloodless" conquest because the Democracies finally realized his true ambitions.

**1939** Hitler, who believed that Germany would lose a war if she had to fight on two major fronts at the same time, made a non-aggression pact with Soviet Russia. Knowing Germany would eventually attack her, the Soviet Union did this to gain time in which to build up her own army.

**1939** At last the Nazis struck. In a four-weeks' compaign the Germans demonstrated their bold strategy of a lightning war of movement (Blitzkrieg) which combined the destructive power of tanks, high-velocity ground weapons, and aircraft. Poland was the first nation to fall.

**1939** Britain and France declared war on Germany, but were unable to give Poland much aid. In the West the two Democracies put their armies into the field and waited for the Germans to strike.

**1940** After months of nervous inactivity that came to be known as the "phoney" war, or "Sitzkrieg," Hitler ordered the attack on France. Within a month the French surrendered, but the British were gallantly able to save 320,000 of their soldiers at Dunkirk, although all their heavy equipment had to be abandoned. The Democracies had bitterly learned that defense alone could not win a modern war.

**1940** Hitler's air force — bombing people, factories, and ports — failed to break either the British spirit or their defenses. This made it impossible for the Germans to invade the island across the Channel. Instead, Hitler soon pushed into the Balkans and overran Yugoslavia and Greece, the only nations who resisted the Nazi onslaught. Treacherous Governments in Rumania, Hungary, and Bulgaria formed alliances with the Nazis.

**1941** The United States, determined to prevent the extinction of the one country which stood between her and the Germans, began Lend-Lease to help Britain with war materials.

**1941** Hitler had always known that to rule the world he would have to crush the United States, but to do that it would be necessary for him to have the natural wealth and industry of Soviet Russia. In June he ordered over 2,000,000 men to the attack. Having as their immediate aim the destruction of the Soviet military forces, the Germans plunged ahead in three directions toward Leningrad, Moscow, and Kiev. But the Red Army retreated skilfully, keeping itself intact although it suffered great loss. By the end of the year, the Ukrainian farmlands, the coal, iron, manganese, and hydro-electric development of the Dnieper bend, and the Donets industrial area were under Nazi control.

**1941** Meeting aboard ship in the North Atlantic, President Roosevelt and British Prime Minister Churchill framed the Atlantic Charter. It pledged their countries to work toward a free world that should be peaceful and propserous.

**1941** Attacked at Pearl Harbor by Japan, Germany's ally, the United States declared war on that Asiatic aggressor on December 8. For over a year the far-seeing American Government had been training an army of peacetime selectees, but compared with our enemies we were poorly prepared.

**1941** Four days after Pearl Harbor, Hitler and Mussolini, who now brought into the open the final part of their plans to destroy Democracy and dominate the world, went to war with the United States. A few hours later Congress answered the challenge made by the European dictators: we were at war with fascist Italy, Germany, and Japan.

# PRE-WAR EUROPE AND ASIA

# GLOSSARY

## SIMPLE EXPLANATIONS OF MILITARY TERMS

ABATIS

An obstacle consisting of trees felled or placed with their branches toward the enemy; often interlaced with barbed wire. See page 43.

ARMAMENT

The arms of troops, or the weapons carried or mounted in a vehicle, plane, or vessel.

ARMOR

A defensive covering, usually of metal, used to give protection against weapons of all kinds.

ARSENAL

A plant where Ordnance materiel is manufactured, stored, and repaired.

AZIMUTH

See page 51.

ASSEMBLY

A unit made up of a number of parts fitted together, not easily disassembled, e.g.: Barrel and receiver assembly for 1903 Rifle; the barrel is ordinarily disassembled from the receiver only at an arsenal.

BALLISTICS

The science that deals with the motion of a projectile, both in the bore of the weapon and after leaving the muzzle, e.g.: the science of ballistics would determine the amount of powder which, for a particular gun and projectile, is necessary to give a certain muzzle velocity.

BATTERY

(1) An Artillery organization similar to a company, which uses a specified number of artillery weapons, usually four. A group of artillery weapons under one command.
(2) An artillery weapon is said to be "In Battery" when the counterrecoil movement has been completed.

BREECH

The rear end of the tube or barrel of a weapon.

CALIBER

(1) In Small Arms, the diameter of the bore of a gun measured between the lands. One caliber equals one inch.
(2) In Artillery, caliber expresses the ratio between the length of the gun tube and the bore diameter measured in similar units.

CAM

An inclined or eccentric surface which imparts motion to another part bearing upon it, by sliding contact.

CARRIAGE

The mount which furnishes support for a cannon in firing, and, in the case of mobile artillery, enables the weapon to be moved readily from one position to another.

CHAMBER

That part of the breech of a cannon which holds the propelling charge.

CONTOUR LINE

See page 53.

COUNTERRECOIL

The return movement of a weapon which occurs after recoil.

DEPOT

A place organized for receiving, storing, inspecting and issuing military supplies.

DETONATOR

A tube containing a sensitive high explosive, used to set off an explosive charge.

DIRECT FIRE

Fire conducted when the target is visible from the gun position.

ECHELON

(1) Echelons of command: Steps in the organization of command, e.g.:
   Platoon
      Company
         Battalion
            Regiment
               etc.
(2) Echelons of maintenance: Steps in the organization of maintenance units.
(3) Echelons of formations:

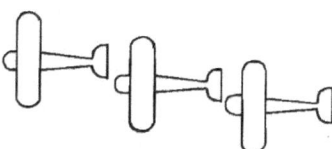

ELEVATION

(1) Height above sea level.
(2) The vertical angle to which the muzzle of a cannon is raised.

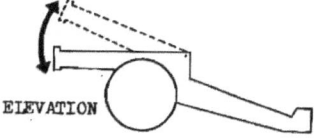

EMPLACEMENT

A prepared position from which a unit or weapon executes its fire mission.

## FIRE-CONTROL EQUIPMENT

Equipment used to direct artillery fire -- not attached to the weapon.

## GRID

A system of parallel and perpendicular lines dividing a map into squares to facilitate rapid location of points.

## GROUP

A unit made up of a number of parts fitted together, easily disassembled, e.g.: bolt group for 1903 rifle, includes firing pin, extractor, mainspring, etc.

## GUN

See Artillery, page 89.

## HOWITZER

See Artillery, page 89.

## INDIRECT FIRE

Fire conducted when the target is not visible from the gun position.

## MAGAZINE

(1) That part of a small arm into which cartridges are placed preparatory to being loaded into the chamber.

(2) A storehouse for ammunition.

## MAINTENANCE

The tasks performed to keep materiel in good working order.

## MORTAR

See Artillery, page 89.

## MUZZLE

The front end of the tube or barrel of a weapon.

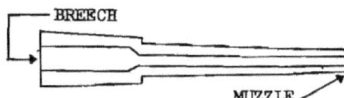

## MUZZLE VELOCITY

The speed (usually expressed as feet per second) with which a projectile leaves the muzzle of a weapon.

## NOMENCLATURE

A system of names. The Ordnance Department publishes a catalog including Standard Nomenclature Lists which give the names of major items, such as guns, ammunition, and vehicles and their component parts.

## ORDNANCE MATERIEL

The general name for equipment supplied by the Ordnance Department.

## PARAPET

A wall or elevation of earth or other material thrown up in front of a trench or emplacement for protection from enemy fire and observation.

## PIECE

A weapon, such as a pistol, rifle or cannon.

## PRIME MOVER

A motor, engine, etc., which furnishes the power for operating machinery of any kind, or for moving other machines, or equipment.

## RAILHEAD

That point along a railroad where supplies are unloaded for transfer to other means of transportation. Supplies may move both to the front and to the rear through railheads.

## RANGE EFFECTIVE

The maximum distance at which a weapon may be aimed and fired with damaging effect.

## RECOIL

The backward movement of a weapon caused by the forces of discharge.

## RIFLING

The spiral grooves cut in the bore of a gun for the purpose of imparting a rotary motion to the projectile.

## ROUND

A round of ammunition consists of all the component parts necessary to fire a weapon once.

## SIGHTING EQUIPMENT

Equipment used in aiming — attached to the weapon.

## SNL

Standard Nomenclature Lists. See Nomenclature.

## STABILIZER

A mechanical device designed to prevent a body from departing from a condition of steady motion or position, or, in case such a motion or position is disturbed, to restore it.

## TERRAIN

A portion of the ground or surface of the earth.

## TRAJECTORY

The path of a projectile in flight.

## TRAVERSE

The lateral change of direction in which a cannon points.

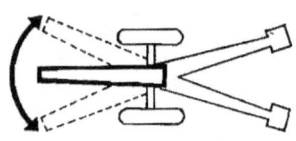

TRAVERSE

## TRITON BLOCK

A block of compressed TNT.

©2013 Periscope Film LLC
All Rights Reserved
ISBN#978-1-937684-18-1
www.PeriscopeFilm.com

www.ingramcontent.com/pod-product-compliance
Lightning Source LLC
LaVergne TN
LVHW061345060426
835512LV00012B/2571